In a world where skepticism is at an all-time high, Christians and non-Christians alike have pressing questions about Christianity that oftentimes go unanswered. In this groundbreaking work, Dr. Bobby Conway brings simplicity to some of the most common questions people ask about Christianity. This is a must-have resource for those who are questioning their own faith, as well as for those who want to become stronger at defending it. I encourage you to buy two copies of this book—one for yourself and one for a friend.

> **ALLEN PARR,** Christian YouTuber, founder of Let's Equip, and author of *Misled: 7 Lies That Distort the Gospel (and How You Can Discern the Truth)*

Not only does Christianity still make sense, so does Pastor Bobby Conway! I doubt you're going to find more succinct and practical answers to the modern objections to Christianity than you'll find in this book. Highly recommended for everyone, but especially for young people who are being bombarded by deceitful messages and harmful ideologies.

> **FRANK TUREK,** president of CrossExamined.org and coauthor of *I Don't Have Enough Faith to Be an Atheist*

Bobby Conway writes from such a genuine, humble place of wanting to help others work through the same challenges he's faced—and that shines through on every page. His transparency is truly refreshing. This book will be a great help to anyone looking for succinct, easy-to-understand, and biblically-sound answers to some of culture's most pressing questions.

> **NATASHA CRAIN,** speaker, podcaster, and author of four books, including *Faithfully Different*

Bobby Conway is one of the most honest truth seekers I know. He shares the personal doubts and questions he has wrestled with in his life, but also the compelling reasons he remains a Christian. This book has depth, but it's also accessible, interesting, and honest.

SEAN MCDOWELL, associate professor of apologetics at Biola University and coauthor of *Evidence for Jesus*

DOES CHRISTIANITY STILL MAKE SENSE?

DOES CHRISTIANITY STILL MAKE SENSE?

A FORMER SKEPTIC RESPONDS TO TODAY'S TOUGHEST OBJECTIONS TO CHRISTIANITY

Bobby Conway

TYNDALE
elevate™
ask. seek. find.

Visit Tyndale online at tyndale.com.

Tyndale and Tyndale's quill logo are registered trademarks of Tyndale House Ministries. Tyndale Elevate and the Tyndale Elevate logo are trademarks of Tyndale House Ministries. Tyndale Elevate is a nonfiction imprint of Tyndale House Publishers, Carol Stream, Illinois.

Does Christianity Still Make Sense? A Former Skeptic Responds to Today's Toughest Objections to Christianity

Cover photograph of bust of Christ, public domain image from The MET on Rawpixel.com.

Author photograph copyright © 2022 by Tim Hull. All rights reserved.

Cover design by Libby Dykstra

Published in association with the literary agency of Mark Sweeney & Associates, Carol Stream, Illinois.

For information about special discounts for bulk purchases, please contact Tyndale House Publishers at csresponse@tyndale.com, or call 1-855-277-9400.

Library of Congress Cataloging-in-Publication Data

A catalog record for this book is available from the Library of Congress.

ISBN 978-1-4964-7643-2

Printed in the United States of America

30	29	28	27	26	25	24
7	6	5	4	3	2	1

CONTENTS

The radio technician pressed a button on his computer console as Bobby Conway and I waited for the caller's question. I was Bobby's guest cohost for this episode of his daily broadcast, a show offering answers to listeners' questions on all matters of faith and Christian living.

"Can you help me understand why God would allow so much evil in the world?"

The caller's question was one I had answered many times in the past, especially when I had been a homicide detective in Los Angeles County.

Bobby looked over and nodded for me to respond. I talked about the reasons God might allow any form of evil, carefully crafting my philosophical case for God's omnipotence, omniscience, and omnibenevolence. Several minutes later, I closed my response by summarizing five or six theological points. I nodded back to Bobby, expecting him to add to my case.

He didn't. Instead, he asked the caller, "Tell me what's happening in your life that's got you asking this question."

That's Bobby Conway. Though he was fully capable of making a philosophical or theological case for God's existence despite the problem of evil, he addressed the *questioner* rather than the *question*.

John Steinbeck once wrote, "You can only understand people if you feel them in yourself."[1] Bobby could *feel* the caller that day. He understood the question because he had empathy for the caller's journey. Few radio hosts are as well-equipped as Bobby is to respond to people *and* their questions in this way.

Bobby has been very transparent about his life, his faith, his failures, and his successes. He is *real*. He has empathy *and* knowledge, compassion *and* wisdom. That's why his answers are accessible and practical—on the radio and in this book.

Does Christianity Still Make Sense? is more than an information book. It's a wisdom book written by a man who has genuinely struggled with the questions, wrestled with his doubts, and emerged faithfully on the other side. He understands you. He's been there. This book is a collection of his questions as well as *yours*.

So start a journey through the most important questions you'll ever ask and allow Bobby Conway to guide your heart and mind.

You're in good hands.

J. WARNER WALLACE,
Dateline-featured cold-case detective, author, speaker, and senior fellow at the Colson Center for Christian Worldview

INTRODUCTION

Every age has had its darkness and its dangers.
The task of the Christian is not to whine
about the moment in which he or she lives
but to understand its problems and respond
appropriately to them.

CARL R. TRUEMAN

Does Christianity still make sense?

Years after I became a Christian, this question haunted me. Even though by then I was the pastor of a large, thriving church and had developed a national reputation as a Christian apologist through my YouTube videos, *The One Minute Apologist*, it seemed as if my entire belief structure was being systematically dismantled. Had I been duped? For an agonizing season of life, it certainly felt that way.

Perhaps you can relate. Maybe you find yourself questioning the sensibility of a faith that once made sense to you. If so, this book is for you. Even if your faith feels solid and secure, this book can equip you to address more than twenty common questions confronting the church today.

To many, it feels as if the church, like the post-iceberg *Titanic*, is quickly sinking, and that many so-called followers of Jesus are jumping ship into a cultural lifeboat. Yet the promise Jesus made long ago still stands: "I will build my church, and all the powers of hell will not conquer it."[1] This is encouraging news for faithful Christians; but if we're being honest, it sometimes appears as if the powers of hell are prevailing.

Why are so many Christians struggling to make sense of Christianity right now?

Among several reasons we could list, many current cultural perspectives make it hard for believers to stand confident in their beliefs. Internally, the church has a serious credibility problem, as some high-profile scandals have damaged our perceived integrity. Combine that with a less-than-favorable reputation for being non-accepting and oppressive, especially to those who fail to conform to a particular moral paradigm, and it can start to feel as if God's good news doesn't have much appeal in our culture.

Certain external objections have also been amplified in our pluralistic society through the emergence of social media. For example, it can be difficult for Christians to maintain that Jesus is the only way to salvation when interacting daily with seemingly nice people who don't believe it. Add to this the claim from some in the scientific community that God is an unnecessary hypothesis, and the age-old problems of evil and suffering, and it's no wonder some Christians feel overwhelmed by the onslaught of questions about their faith.

Maybe you're wondering whether there are credible answers to these abundant objections. I believe there are, but that doesn't mean the cultural critics don't have some fair criticisms, especially as it pertains to the scandals of recent years. But their objections aren't enough to sink the church. Sure, we've been battered by many self-inflicted wounds, but there's still a way forward—which I will show you in the following pages by offering a compass aimed at true north. No doubt these are challenging times, but now is not the time to jump ship. Rather, it's time for Christians to slow down, reflect, and do some necessary repair work—renewing our vision of the good news of the gospel in the face of a hostile culture.

In the chapters ahead, I will address some of the hardest-hitting questions Christians face in today's culture, as well as some of the recurring questions that seem to pop up in every generation. But before we get to the questions and answers, I invite you to join me on a brief journey through my own story—from unbelief to belief, then to near-unbelief, and finally back to belief again. My motivation in giving you a glimpse beneath the cover of my own life is to help you better grasp the gravity of what it meant for me to think that I might fall away from the Christian faith after having been rescued from a life of recklessness and despair as a young man. And how I went from being an apologist committed to defending Christianity to a doubter wondering whether it still made sense, and then back to having a solid assurance of faith.

For you to fully understand the implications of the question, *Does Christianity still make sense?*, it will require some context, because my story didn't unravel overnight. Change is often best depicted through contrasts, and contrasts are at the heart of my story—from prodigal to pastor; from apologist to near apostate; from relapse to recovery to fully alive again! I certainly don't expect you to relate to my story in full, and maybe you won't relate to any of it. But here's what I know: There are many hurting doubters out there who need to hear a story of someone who made it through years of doubt and is able to exclaim with confidence, "Christianity *still* makes sense."

You hold in your hands a resource for people who have been crushed under the weight of doubt; a vital resource for those deconstructing Christianity or pondering a departure from the faith. In part 2, I address more than twenty contemporary challenges to Christianity under five broad categories: (1) church scandals; (2) the claim that the church is nonaccepting; (3) the problem of why there is suffering and evil in the world; (4) the issue of whether Jesus is the only way to salvation; and (5) various scientific objections. These questions aren't the only ones you'll hear in our culture, but they address some of the key challenges that Christians face today.

After responding to these concerns, I bring the book full circle in a closing chapter titled "Why Christianity Still Makes Sense to Me," followed by a special afterword titled, "A Way Forward for the Church," where I put on my pastoral hat and offer practical advice for those interested in missional ways to engage our ever-changing culture. I also address the desperate need for a new reformation within the church and offer four crucial action steps we can take toward that objective. In the end, it is my hope and prayer that what I've written will encourage you to stay on the one true ship—the church of Jesus Christ—that can safely carry you home.

PART I

A JOURNEY TOWARD SOMEWHERE

I
LIFE WITHOUT GOD

All our fret and worry is caused by
calculating without God.

OSWALD CHAMBERS

As crazy as it may sound, I never heard the gospel until I was
nineteen. Growing up, I was clueless about all things Christian. I
never wondered about the true meaning of Christmas or Easter.
I knew the Bible was supposed to be a sacred book of some kind,
but I had no idea why. I certainly wasn't familiar with its contents.
Names like David, Abraham, Noah, and Moses had no context or
association for me. Even Jesus didn't resonate. If you had asked me
who he was, I might have said, "You mean the guy who looks like
he's wearing a diaper on that cross?" Beyond that, nothing.

How could that happen in America? I'm not sure, but it happened to me.

I do remember going to church a few times with my parents,
but we weren't "church people." Dad had grown up Catholic and
Mom Protestant, and when they got married, they could never

align, so we pretty much avoided church altogether. My dad's parents were devout Catholics, but they never spoke about their faith. I went with them to Mass on a few occasions, but I was a fish out of water. I do remember, however, the maple-frosted, peanut-covered donuts they served there.

Don't get me wrong, it's not like I was an atheist. That worldview always felt untenable to me. The idea that the entire universe emerged out of nothing and that people evolved from apes seemed absurd. I just didn't buy it. So, it wasn't that I didn't believe in God. I did. It's just that I had no idea who God was. I do, however, recall sensing God's presence once when I was spending the summer with my maternal grandparents in Southfield, Michigan. For whatever reason, I found myself praying one day. I don't remember what I said, but I do recall being overwhelmed with an amazing sense of peace. So much so that, after I was done praying, I asked my grandmother, "Does praying feel good?" "It does," she replied.

Like most kids in the 1970s and 1980s, I spent my childhood roaming the neighborhood, playing pickup games and going on long bike rides. The one thing I despised more than anything was school. Oh, how I hated sitting in a classroom!

Though I didn't have the words for it as a kid, I clearly struggled with anxiety and a bad case of attention-deficit disorder (now called ADHD). To say that ADHD made it difficult for me to concentrate in class would be a major understatement. I have more memories of staring at the large white clock on the wall than I have of doing homework. My relationship with books as a kid was nonexistent. I could read, but my ADHD got in the way of comprehending or retaining anything I read, mostly because I found reading to be hopelessly boring. No joke, I don't recall reading a single book growing up besides Judy Blume's *Freckle Juice*, which reads at a second- or third-grade level. What I thought of books can be summarized by the fact that on one occasion I was sent home from school for gluing the pages of a book together in class while the rest of the students quietly read.

If my ADHD made it hard for me to enjoy school, my anxiety made me uncomfortable in my own skin. I was always apprehensive, and mostly for no good reason. I hated it, eventually turning to alcohol when I was fifteen, which was like discovering liquid gold. At last I had found a way to cope with my anxiety.

As you might imagine, I soon progressed beyond alcohol to the world of drugs, and eventually to LSD—through which I hoped to find myself, like the hippies before my day. I remember sitting around with some friends, journals in hand, listening to Pink Floyd's *The Wall* as we sought to unlock the existential meaning of life. Eventually, I reached a point where all I could think about was the next party or the next fix. One night, while walking along the Santa Cruz boardwalk, I came across a drug dealer who was selling LSD for two bucks a hit. I didn't have any cash, so I asked whether he would take a check. He said he would, so I wrote him a $2.00 check and off I went.

As my high school years were coming to a close, my inattentiveness to life began catching up with me. With the alcohol and drugs, along with lying, cheating, stealing, family arguments, car wrecks, and promiscuity, I had really made a mess of my life. I was looking for meaning, but in all the wrong places.

I had also become quite accustomed to failure, having literally failed several classes in high school, including driver's ed and PE. How does someone fail PE? By not showing up for class. Nevertheless, I knew I had to make some sort of career decision upon graduation. If there was one thing I knew, it was that the traditional learning route was not for me. So I chose the next best thing: The Few. The Proud. The Marines. Or at least I hoped to.

When Operation Desert Storm broke out during my senior year, I was determined to enlist. I hopped in the car and drove thirty miles to the US Marine Corps recruiting office in San Jose to inform them of my readiness for war. I even let them know that I could bypass boot camp to get into action sooner.

After the recruiters had a good long laugh, I left dejected and began to prepare for the required Armed Services Vocational Aptitude Battery, the weed-out test for all enlistees. Unfortunately, I failed to meet the Marines' high-bar entrance standard of a 31, and I had to wait thirty days to take the test again. But it didn't matter, because I failed that one too, scoring a whopping 27. (And here my biggest fear had been that I wouldn't pass the drug test.) Fortunately, though the Army required a 28 to enter their lowest-level infantry, they offered me a waiver. But even that didn't help when I failed the physical due to a past knee injury.

With my military dreams now thoroughly destroyed, I decided to enroll at a local community college. But I had no idea what was required. I thought you took some classes of your own choosing for a few years and then were awarded a degree. Eventually I learned the difference between required courses and electives, but I was aimless, and I knew it. On top of that, I was wracked with guilt for making such a mess of things.

At this point in my life, there were two things I knew I needed: a sense of purpose and a way to get rid of my guilt.

2

STRUGGLING TO LIVE FOR JESUS

We must . . . allow the Holy Spirit to break our hearts and create a passion for Christ . . . of such a nature that the things of this world will begin to diminish in their attraction for us.

A. W. TOZER

Around the time I finished high school, my dad was offered a new job and my parents moved back to Southern California, where we had lived when I was younger. I decided to tag along, hoping for a fresh start in the next chapter of my life. I enrolled at Saddleback Community College and was offered a spot on their baseball team. Baseball had been the one thing that kept me from completely imploding during high school. One of my teammates at Saddleback, a guy named Cade, was an outspoken Christian, and we quickly hit it off. He was really the first Christian I had ever known. I knew I needed to change my trajectory a bit, so I decided to give up drugs and cigarettes and limit myself to drinking, dipping snuff, and, of course, flirting with the girls.

When I met Cade, I learned that he had lost his younger brother to leukemia about a year earlier, and I was impressed by his ability to cope with life after such a great loss. I'm sure it was difficult for him to spend time with me. He was straitlaced, and I should have been in a straitjacket. As our friendship grew, he talked to me about Jesus, and I grilled him nonstop with questions. Eventually, he invited me to church at Calvary Chapel in Costa Mesa. This was the church where the Jesus Movement had really gained traction in the late 1960s. I'm not sure how long it took before I agreed to attend, but at some point I did. And what I found there was surprisingly refreshing.

Cade had told me about a local pastor named Greg Laurie who spoke on Monday nights at Calvary Chapel. Laurie spoke from the Bible in a way that made sense to me—and he used my vernacular, leveraging words like *dude, bro, cool,* and *stoked.* More importantly, he shared how Jesus had come to take away our guilt and offer us life purpose—precisely the two answers I was searching for. His preaching was contagious, and I couldn't wait to go again the next week. The music was great, too. Contemporary and understandable. What didn't make sense to me was why so many people raised their hands during the songs. I wasn't ready yet for "expressive worship," but overall I sensed that these people had something that was missing in my life. I don't recall how long it took, but one Monday night I found myself at the altar ready to receive Jesus.

My early discipleship, courtesy of Cade, included watching old-school VHS cartoon tapes featuring stories like Daniel and the lions' den; Shadrach, Meshach, and Abednego; and the parting of the Red Sea. Crazily enough, I ate this stuff up. I even got myself a big cross to wear outside my shirt. The kind that people would see and conclude, "He must make Jesus proud." I also purchased a bumper sticker for my car that said "Jesus Died 4 U." That was great until I had a road-rage incident with another driver on the freeway. As I rolled down my window to flip him the bird, I suddenly remembered my bumper sticker. Fortunately, I was able to recover quickly and offer a gentle wave instead.

What was happening to me?

At Cade's suggestion, I got myself a new student Bible, but of course I had no idea how to read it. I kid you not, if Greg Laurie would have said, "Turn to Romans for today's message," I would've thought, *Bummer, I didn't bring Romans; I brought my Bible.* And then there was all this talk about the forefathers. I had kind of picked up on Abraham, Isaac, and Jacob, but for the longest time I was wondering who the fourth one was.

"Oh, it's *fore*fathers!"

Yep, thick as a brick.

As excited as I was to have my sins forgiven and be in a personal relationship with Jesus, I didn't realize what I was up against. Coming to Jesus didn't magically take away my strong desire to party. Learning to live the Christian life was a real wrestling match for me. My feelings had been my lifelong master, and it was hard to ignore them. The first few years of my Christian walk were marked by lots of promises to quit alcohol and promiscuous living, followed by numerous failures. I had the desire to follow Jesus, but the desire to drink and mess around with girls was stronger. Like the time I attended one of Greg Laurie's Harvest Crusade events at Anaheim Stadium. I worshiped, listened, and felt challenged to live differently, but as soon as I left the stadium, I pulled off at a liquor store in Santa Ana and bought a twelve-pack of beer. Madness.

This obviously hurt my witness for Christ. Like the time I was headed to a party sporting my new Harvest Crusade T-shirt. I stopped off at a liquor store in Mission Viejo to pick up a keg to contribute. As I was walking out, a guy entering the liquor store noticed my T-shirt and the massive keg of beer I was carrying.

"Nice Christian," he said.

With my hypocrisy on full display, I sought to cover my shame with what I thought was a brilliant response: "Well, Jesus drank wine." Bad answer, Bobby.

By the end of my time at Saddleback Community College, I had bluffed and cheated my way into an associate of arts degree and managed to get accepted at Chico State, a school ranked by MTV and *Playboy* magazine as the number-one party school in the country. Not the wisest choice, by far. But of course I convinced myself that things would be different this time. I was going to shine for Jesus.

My internal conflict can be illustrated by the cross I used to wear around my neck. On party nights, I didn't take it off, but I tucked it inside my shirt so as not to be seen as a sham for Christ. The sense of guilt was palpable, but the desire to drink was, sadly, more intense. Upon my arrival at Chico State—without a vehicle, by the way, because I had sold my VW Scirocco and had drunk away the profits—I caved almost immediately. Maybe Jesus and I could pick things up at another time; for now, I was going to make the most of my college experience.

I got a student loan, but I used the money to buy booze. I think I made it to class a half-dozen times that first semester before I blew the one shot I had left to keep things together: making the baseball team. After three surgeries in the past three years resulting from injuries, things weren't looking good. I knew I had to take my tryout seriously. To avoid the temptation to drink at my apartment on the weekend before the Monday tryout, I drove three hours away. I needed to keep a level head.

Unfortunately, that didn't work either. Once I arrived at my destination, I convinced myself I needed a drink, and off to the races I went. When tryouts came on Monday and it was my turn to showcase my skills, I put the final nail in the coffin of my career with an unforgettable pitch—throwing the ball over the backstop. Yes, you read that correctly. I was done. Loser. Afterward, I stood behind the backstop with my cleats hanging over my shoulder and thought, *What am I doing with my life?* I had hit rock bottom, but this time I knew I needed help.

In desperation, I went to the campus counseling center to talk to someone about alcoholism, and they encouraged me to check in to a recovery program. I thought about it long and hard and set a date for nine days later. Then I promptly went on a nine-day bender, "to get the cravings out of my system."

On the appointed night, I arrived at rehab as the youngest one in the room, and the people there began teaching me how to live a life of sobriety. It was difficult, especially because my roommate woke me up like clockwork every morning, coughing loudly after taking a massive bong hit. On top of that, our pad was the drop-in place for anyone looking for a fix. I had to get out of there—and fast.

In recovery, there is a saying that goes, "Sometimes you need to change your people, places, and playthings." That resonated with me, but where could I go? Fortunately, an old party friend from high school, Dave, was living in Fayetteville, Arkansas, and he invited me to room with him. I told him I was getting my life together, which meant no more partying. He agreed, and soon I was off to the Ozarks.

3

THE LAND OF OPPORTUNITY

If you want a change in your life, if you want forgiveness and peace and joy that you've never known before, God demands total surrender. He becomes the Lord and the ruler of your life.

BILLY GRAHAM

Not long after my arrival in Arkansas in January 1995, Dave introduced me to the woman who would become my wife. Like me, Heather was a new Christian, and we quickly hit it off. Due to various circumstances, after six months I ended up moving back to California, and Heather decided to follow me. I got my old job back at the Ritz Carlton in Dana Point, where I had worked as a valet parking attendant during my days at Saddleback College. But this time around I was truly on fire for Jesus, and people noticed. My fellow employees even nicknamed me The Reverend. On one occasion, I got into trouble for tuning all the radios in the cars I parked to the Christian station KWAVE. Apparently, the guests didn't like the valet driver toying with their radios. Soon, I was promoted to bellman, but not before the powers that be felt assured I wouldn't witness to the guests as I checked them in to their rooms.

On nights when Heather and I weren't working, we were at one church event or another at Saddleback Church, which had a thriving recovery program called Celebrate Recovery that became a game changer for me. Life was exciting, and I was finally experiencing the joy of being set free from my addiction. Though no longer haunted by pervasive guilt, I still had a gnawing question about my life's purpose.

I didn't realize it at the time, but the direction of my life was about to change forever as I fully surrendered myself to God.

During a graveyard shift at the hotel, as I was backing a car into a parking spot, I noticed a license plate on the car in front of me that read MATT419. I locked onto it and found myself repeating, "MATT419, MATT419." Then I sensed the Holy Spirit prompting me, "Go get your Bible and look up Matthew 4:19." I quickly ran back to my desk and turned to the verse in my Bible: "'Come, follow me,' Jesus said, 'and I will make you fishers of men.'" Blown away, I stepped outside, lay down on my back, and gazed into the star-studded sky as I surrendered my life to full-time ministry.

At this stage in my life, I still knew very little about the Bible, and perhaps that's why in those early years God directed me so often through powerful circumstantial moments, such as noticing the license plate on a car. Whatever this connection meant, I knew that I needed to get prepared if I was going to enter the ministry. God had given me a vision, but now I needed to grow into it.

As I was trying to decide between Calvary Chapel Bible College in Southern California and Central Baptist College in Conway, Arkansas, I was torn and needed clarity. Heather was going home to Arkansas to complete her degree at a university just a stone's throw from Central Baptist, so that certainly seemed enticing. But I didn't want to make my decision based on that one factor alone.

So I eagerly sought God's direction, and I distinctly remember pleading with him for an answer.

After praying, I met up with Heather to attend the Purpose Driven Church conference at Saddleback. There must have been two thousand pastors in attendance, from all over the world. As we came to the end of a praise song, the worship pastor asked all the participants to greet one another. To my right was a man named Kirk. His badge said he lived in Redwood, Texas. When I introduced him to Heather, who was sitting to my left, he immediately noticed her accent and asked, "Where are you from?" When Heather replied, "Arkansas," what Kirk said next absolutely floored me.

"Oh yeah, I used to live in Arkansas. I lived in a town called Conway, north of Little Rock, and I went to a tiny little Bible college you probably never heard of: Central Baptist College."

I was speechless. I mean, that very morning I had been asking God whether I should stay in Southern California or go to Central Baptist College in Arkansas, and now Kirk, a current resident of Texas, had picked up on my Arkansas girlfriend's accent and told me he had gone to that exact school. Say what you will, but as I sit here today writing this chapter, I am still amazed at God's providential leading. For me, the answer could not have been any clearer.

The night before we left California, I proposed to Heather, and my new fiancée and I were off once again to the Land of Opportunity. This time, however, I had a clear purpose.

The culture shock I experienced in Arkansas was comedic at times. I still laugh when I picture myself showing up in the land of camouflage and hiking boots and trying to fit in with my board shorts and Vans. It took some time.

And then there was the college itself. At first, I couldn't figure out why everybody called everyone else "brother." There was

Brother Doug, Brother John, Brother Darrell, and so on. I soon learned that it was a Baptist thing, but it felt a little weird to me, so I just told people to call me Bro Bobby.

Meanwhile, my academic limitations soon became obvious. No longer could I rely on my masterful cheating skills to get passing grades. It was time to learn. I couldn't even remember what an adjective was, so I learned English grammar by taking Greek. At times I had to pay someone to type my papers because I'd never learned to type. I spent most of my time studying and going to the nearby university to share Christ with the students there. And at the end of fall semester, Heather and I got married.

Through the years, I've been asked how I got into apologetics in the first place. The answer is quite simple: by actively engaging in evangelism. During my campus witnessing days, I was stumped on more than one occasion by people's questions. So I would study up to keep it from happening again. The way I see it, anyone who claims that apologetics isn't important has just revealed how little evangelism he or she is doing.

On top of street witnessing and open-air preaching, I got involved with a nursing home ministry that I found I really loved. Each week, I'd visit the elderly, play some old hymns from my boom box, and present a simple gospel message. Those were some good times. My burden for evangelism was so intense that I even started randomly calling people in the local phone book to see whether they knew Jesus. My goal was to get through the entire phone book, which of course never happened; but the desire to see people saved weighed heavily on me.

Three years after arriving in Arkansas, I graduated, and I wept like a baby at God's faithfulness and the life change he had brought about in me. During this stint, I was even awarded an outstanding Christian character award. God certainly has a sense of humor.

Following graduation, Heather and I had some decisions to make. We had a newborn baby girl, and it was tempting to settle in to a ministry position with what I had. But we both knew I needed more academic training. So, about eighteen months after graduation, and with our second child on the way, we headed off to Dallas Theological Seminary in Texas, where I could earn a four-year master's in theology. This delay was hard for a guy anxious to begin full-time ministry, but deep down I knew that if anyone needed the extra training, it was me. During my seminary years, I studied eight hours a day, six days a week. It was like drinking water from a fire hose. I was consumed with the academic life.

Dallas, however, was also where I had my first encounter with doubt. While taking a course on the Gospels with the esteemed professor J. Dwight Pentecost, I was tasked with reading a harmony of the Gospels. Examining the Gospels side by side makes it easy to detect similarities and differences. This project turned out to be a challenge for me, as I began to notice more apparent discrepancies than I felt equipped to resolve. Fortunately, the battle was short-lived, as I devised a way to reconcile what I was reading. But this would not be the end of my doubts; down the road, they would return in spades.

4

FREEDOM FROM THE VENGEANCE OF DOUBT

If ours is an examined faith, we should be unafraid to doubt.... There is no believing without some doubting, and believing is all the stronger for understanding and resolving doubt.

OS GUINNESS

In 2004, after seminary, our family relocated to Charlotte, North Carolina, to plant a church, where we served for the next fourteen years. Not long after arriving, I entered a doctoral program in apologetics at the nearby seminary started by famed apologist Norman Geisler. By this time, I was flourishing academically. In fact, I graduated from the program summa cum laude (with highest distinction). This was a surreal moment, to say the least, and I was humbled by what God had done in my life. Shortly after graduation, I launched a YouTube program called the *One Minute Apologist*, where I started developing videos to address the various apologetic questions Christians may encounter.

This was enjoyable and nerve-wracking at the same time. It was fun because I was getting to meet and interview some of the world's best Christian apologists. It was also challenging in that I didn't have a clue about YouTube or how to maximize the platform, as it was all so new. On top of this, the church we had planted was growing. Plus I was writing books, speaking around the country, and starting to exhibit early signs of burnout. For the previous several years, education had consumed my life. Looking back, I can see how I simply applied my addictive personality to my studies. I had been obsessing for years about learning, and it was beginning to take its toll. So, like any good addict, I decided to enter yet another doctoral program—this time at the prestigious University of Birmingham in England. It was during this season, as I studied in the philosophy of religion department, that my doubts returned—this time with a vengeance.

As you can imagine, this created a lot of internal pressure. Here I was, a pastor leading a large church, and an apologist defending the faith I was now doubting. I wasn't trying to be disingenuous; my ADHD brain was just producing more questions than I had time to process. In some ways, my obsession with learning was turning my Christian walk into one long Q&A session.

This season of doubt lasted for several years and was excruciating beyond words. No longer could I sense God's tangible presence. People would say, "You just need to read the Bible more, Bobby." Though their remarks were well intended, reading the Bible was part of the problem. I had come to dread it for fear of accumulating more doubts.

Truth be told, my doubts had turned me into an empty shell. The young zealot had lost his zeal. I felt as if God had forsaken me. Abandoned. Confused. And, frankly, scared to death. I felt as if I were trapped, alone in a maze without an exit, as if my faith hung by a thread that could be severed at any moment. It got so bad that I started wondering, *Am I going to fall away from the faith?* Though that was never my desire, the struggle was real; Christianity no longer made sense to me, but neither did any other belief system. I felt crushed under the weight of my doubts—and at times I just wanted to escape it all.

What I didn't realize was how doubt can serve as an ingredient in the recipe God uses to make a true believer into an apologist. As I wrestled, I thought about other doubts I would inherit if I were to become an atheist, a Muslim, a Buddhist, or even an agnostic. None of those options appealed to me, though I suppose agnosticism seemed the most benign. But then I reasoned that even many agnostics aren't agnostic about whether there is an explanation for the universe; they simply contend it's impossible to know what it is.

It seemed wiser to give myself fully to what appeared to be the best explanation, rather than spend the rest of my life arguing that it was impossible to fully answer the question. I was vexed, but I also knew that doubt isn't exclusively a Christian problem. It's a human problem. In the absence of certainty, there will always be room for doubt; my question was which worldview best closed the doubt gap. Eventually, I came around to believing that Christianity makes the strongest cumulative case, and I found a way to settle back into my faith. Moreover, God found ways to channel my obsessive brain to help me develop as an apologist, including enabling me to write a book titled *Doubting Toward Faith* to help my fellow doubters.

Ultimately, God did for me what I never could have done for myself. He got me out of the maze. He showed me the exit. He showed me the way home. I'm both thankful and humbled. Certainly, questions and doubts still creep into my head from time to time, but they feel more like honest inquiries than panic-stricken fears. For me, the most reassuring conviction is that Christianity not only *still* makes sense, but it also makes the *best* sense. I learned a lot through my extended mental battle with doubt. As I reflect on the issue, I can identify several contributing factors.

The first was that I had been indoctrinated into a narrow-minded theology. As I've mentioned, when I came to Christ, I wasn't the brightest guy on the block. I realized I knew nothing—which made me very teachable but also caused me to be too trusting. As a result, I committed to theological positions prematurely, before I had time to adequately suss things out. The problem with having a narrow base is that, when further learning exposes alternative positions, it can ignite a crisis of faith.

I think we'd be well advised to expose new believers to the various theological positions held by sincere people within orthodox Christianity instead of trying to indoctrinate them into a particular denominational or theological box. In many ways, that's what denominations are: different size boxes that attempt to establish how large or small Christianity is.

We need doctrinal boundaries, to be sure, but my initial introduction to Christianity was a small-box version of the faith. Whereas some people seem to want to be as conservative about their conservativism as they can be, I want to be as liberal about my conservativism as I can be, without slipping into heresy. When we are overly conservative (and, yes, I realize that some people don't have a category for that), we inevitably alienate others who are well within the lines of orthodox Christianity but whose faith comes in a bigger box. When we are as liberal as we can be about our conservativism, we have room to include others outside our doctrinal preferences who are still part of the body of Christ.

What I needed was a type of doctrinal discipleship that encouraged me not to commit to theological positions too quickly. I needed a version of discipleship that would encourage me to enjoy learning without trying to *conquer* it; one that acknowledged that there are a lot of views out there. I needed to learn how to take my time, study the various positions within orthodoxy, and then commit to positions I believed best express the message of Scripture. In some ways, during my season of doubt, parts of my prior belief system were being deconstructed, but not to the point of becoming "progressive." To me, so-called progressive Christianity is a pseudo-Christianity that has basically left the box altogether.

Another factor that contributed to my doubt was my foolish quest for omniscience. I'm not sure why I ever thought Christianity—or any other belief, for that matter—can eliminate all the mystery. Regardless of whatever faith we choose, we're all finite creatures. Every belief system has its questions; Christians are not alone in that regard. What brought my prolonged season of doubt to a close was not another apologetic argument; it was my returning to the faith of a child. By humbly recognizing my own limitations and willingly trusting God to help me learn to enjoy him again, I was able to reconnect to my faith. Instead of trying to decipher all the answers to my endless list of questions, I was able to exit the maze of doubt that had trapped me for so many years.

As I reflect on that long, dark night of the soul, I recognize many benefits that came from that gut-wrenching season. Though my beliefs still fit firmly within the bounds of orthodoxy, I'm not nearly as black-and-white in my views as I once was. I'm much more charitable to other streams of thought within Christianity. I also feel much better equipped, having gone through that season. After being bombarded with hundreds of doubts that I had to think my way through, I believe that God has given me a better grasp of what makes Christianity so beautifully distinct from other worldviews. I also believe I'm able to live with a greater sense of authenticity, as I no longer fear that some Christians might consign me to a small box, just for thinking more charitably about theological matters and landing outside their comfort zone. And finally, having gone through years of study, I am better armed philosophically to think through my doubts the next time they arise.

It is these types of benefits that I hope you will begin to experience if you are still stuck in the maze. God can bring you out, so don't feel hopeless. Don't give up. And don't fall away. Find encouragement through a story like mine, knowing that, if God can see me through, he can certainly see you through. And if you think you are beyond getting hammered by doubt, be careful. No one is above testing. I was the last person who thought my passionate relationship with Christ could turn so desperately sour. Yet it did. So please take heed.

At the end of this book, after discussing the factors that led to my doubts, and the benefits that resulted, I will reveal the four reasons I didn't walk away from the faith and why Christianity still makes sense to me. I will conclude the book by unveiling the key that ultimately led me out of the maze of doubt. But first it's time to consider several objections our culture presents to us as Christians.

Regardless of whether you relate to my story—or to anyone else's doubts, for that matter—the answers on the following pages can better equip you to make sense of Christianity. The purpose of presenting these questions is not to address the various doubts with which I personally wrestled, but rather to tackle the biggest objections the church faces. But I will be sure to bring my story back into the picture when appropriate, in order to show you how I reconciled those particular splinters in my own mind. That said, let's address some of those objections.

PART II

ANSWERING TODAY'S BIGGEST OBJECTIONS

SCANDALS IN THE CHURCH

5

WHY ARE THERE SO MANY SCANDALS IN THE CHURCH?

If you say that the history of the Church is a long succession of scandals, you are telling the truth, though if that is all you say, you are distorting the truth.

GERALD VANN

My heart broke in 2020 when rumors began to surface that Ravi Zacharias, the famed Christian apologist who had passed away earlier that year, had led a double life, frequently engaging in inappropriate sexual activity. I first caught wind of these reports while I was speaking at a conference in Sacramento, along with one of Ravi's prominent employees. As we were hanging out after the conference, this associate's phone began blowing up with texts about the matter. At the time, none of us believed the allegations. Ravi Zacharias was the last person anyone would think could be guilty of such things. He had built a reputation of such impeccable character that he was given the benefit of the doubt by those who knew and admired him. Everyone was horrified by the very suggestion of impropriety.

In the wake of these reports and the subsequent investigation, we saw Ravi's legacy collapse and Ravi Zacharias International Ministries implode. And yet, sadly enough, the Zacharias scandal is just one of many in recent memory. We've seen international pedophilia scandals rock the Roman Catholic Church; charges of sexual harassment bring down Bill Hybels at Willow Creek; allegations of financial mismanagement and anger issues lead to the firing of James MacDonald at Harvest Bible Chapel; abuse of spiritual authority topple Mark Driscoll at Mars Hill Church in Seattle; and accusations of sexual misconduct lead to the resignation of Hillsong's founding pastor, Brian Houston.

It's no wonder the church is in such a mess. Perhaps you, too, are curious as to why there are so many scandals involving Christian leaders.

If we are going to address this issue, we must begin by acknowledging the ugly truth of these scandals and recognizing the deep pain of anyone confused, angered, or personally affected by them. Denying the problem, or defending bad behavior—by minimizing it, excusing it, or even explaining it away—won't help. When people ask, "Why are there so many scandals in the church?" we can begin by validating their concern. For example, we might say, "That's a fair question, and the situation truly breaks my heart. Many people have been hurt badly by the church. I can only imagine the pain of those who have been directly affected. I'm very sorry if you have been hurt by any of these situations."

So often in apologetics, we start with a defense. But I think it's actually more effective to begin with a concession. Before you try to defend the faith, ask yourself, *Is there something I can first concede?* We're trying to *build* bridges, not burn them. We would do well to acknowledge points of agreement and then make our best defense. That said, here are some ways we can respond to questions about church scandals:

1. *Scandals are not exclusively a church problem; they are a human problem.* Where there are people, there will be scandals. Even among atheists, Mormons, Muslims, Buddhists, Hindus, and agnostics—you name the group, and I can point to a scandal. Unfortunately, we humans are a scandal-prone bunch. That doesn't excuse it, but it gives some perspective.

2. *Just because someone professes to be a Christian doesn't mean he or she is living as a Christian.* Jesus could not have been clearer when he said, "Not everyone who says to me, 'Lord, Lord,' will enter the kingdom of heaven, but only the one who does the will of my Father who is in heaven."[1] The church is full of people who *say* they believe in Jesus, but their lives prove otherwise. I won't pretend to know the human heart on such matters, but Jesus does—and he has already warned us that not everyone who claims to be a Christian really is one. So, what does all this have to do with scandals? Sometimes the church gets a bad rap for the actions of pseudo believers. We have enough baggage of our own; but unfortunately, we also carry the unnecessary baggage of posers.

3. *Just because someone is truly a Christian doesn't mean he or she is exempt from sin.* A lot could be said about the specific causes of scandals in the church—such as hypocrisy, hunger for power, covetousness, greed, lust, abuse, addiction, etc.—and all these actions fall under the category of sin. Just because Christians are forgiven doesn't mean they won't sin. As the saying goes, becoming a Christian doesn't make one *sinless*, but it ought to make one sin *less*. Even so, given our sinful human nature, there isn't a single Christian

who is exempt from the kind of sin that could lead to a church scandal.

4. *Too many Christians are overly influenced by culture and not influenced enough by Scripture.* In our society, we spend countless hours listening to music, watching programs, and interacting with content that runs contrary to Scripture, often failing to recognize how far we've drifted from God's moral standard for our lives. It's no exaggeration to say that many in the church are lucky if they spend thirty minutes a week in the Bible, while taking in thirty to forty *hours* of cultural messaging through music, movies, social media, etc. If anything, I'm being conservative. For many Christians, Bible-reading is basically extinct, and the hours enmeshed with culture are probably double my estimate. It's no wonder the church is ridden with scandals. We've neglected the source of wisdom for how to live the Christian life, and instead we are led by our feelings and intuitions and influenced by sound bites and social media.

These first four points address the issue of personal responsibility. But problems in the church can also arise because of *systemic* problems—especially with how we treat our pastors and what we expect of them.

1. *Deficiencies in training.* Many pastors have a master's-level education but receive no training for how to handle all the on-the-ground issues they will face in ministry: finances, human resources (working with a staff and dealing with personnel issues), counseling or referring people for counseling, setting boundaries, etc.

2. *Celebrity and self-sufficiency.* We too often put pastors on a pedestal, such that they can feel above the need for counseling or accountability. The pastoral gift is only one of the leadership gifts mentioned in Scripture. Some sort of eldership (which has different names in different churches) is also important to create a balanced, mature, and godly leadership structure. When responsibility is shared among a group of wise and mature leaders, it diminishes the chances that any one leader will succumb to the pitfalls of celebrity and self-sufficiency.

3. *Burnout.* We often expect pastors to do it all (see point 1) and to always be available to everyone. But we're not usually as good at providing them with support and resources. Here again, a balanced leadership structure can keep the burden of ministry from falling too heavily on any one person.

4. *Lack of continuing education.* We expect doctors, counselors, teachers, social workers, lawyers, and many other professionals to keep up with continuing education, yet our pastors often get little to no continuing education.

The bottom line is that we must create the proper environment in the church where scandals are less likely to occur—where accountability, preparedness, and *encouragement* are baked in to the system.

Back to the question at hand: As regrettable and reprehensible as scandals are in creating a black eye for the church and bringing dishonor to God, I think we can rightfully ask, "Do scandals negate the truthfulness of Christianity?" I don't think so, and I'll show you why, using a syllogism, a logical argument containing two premises and a conclusion. If the premises are true, it necessarily follows that the conclusion will also be true. Such arguments can be useful in helping us recognize loopholes in our logic.

So, here we go. To claim that scandals disprove Christianity would be equivalent to the following argument:

Premise 1: If scandals exist in the church, then Christianity is not true.
Premise 2: Scandals exist in the church.
Conclusion: Therefore, Christianity is not true.

The problem with this argument is obvious: Premise 1 is a false assertion. Scandals may disappoint us, but they don't negate the truthfulness of Christianity, nor do they provide a good reason to reject Christianity. Nowhere does the Bible attempt to cover up scandals; rather, it recognizes and confronts them head-on. One quick read through the book of 1 Corinthians is enough to show that it didn't take long for the early church to find itself enmeshed in scandal.

Though scandals may hurt the credibility of Christians, they don't hurt the credibility of Jesus. He's the only one who ever lived without moral failure, and consequently he's the only one who can truly forgive us for the sins that lead to our scandals.

Finally, to deny Christianity because of scandals in the church puts too much stock in people. Our hope was never meant to be placed in humanity, but in Christ. People will always let us down. Count on it. If we put too much hope and trust in other people, we will become hopeless in our faith when they let us down. It's high time we traded in our disillusionment with Christians for deeper intimacy with Jesus.

6

AREN'T CHRISTIANS JUST A BUNCH OF HYPOCRITES?

If a person claims to be without sin and then demonstrates sin, surely that person is a hypocrite. But for a Christian simply to demonstrate that he is a sinner does not convict him of hypocrisy.

R. C. SPROUL

When you hear the word *hypocrisy*, what comes to mind? A power-hungry pastor, a corrupt cop, or an abusive spouse? How about an actor in a play? In ancient Greece, actors (*hypokritēs*) wore large masks to depict the characters they played on stage. Over time, the word came to represent a person who acts one way but lives another. Today we call a person who pretends to be moral while living deceptively a hypocrite.

Sadly, one high-profile example of this was Carl Lentz, former pastor of Hillsong NYC, who passed himself off as a sports agent to have an affair with a woman he had met in a city park. When *Vanity Fair*, the *New York Post*, *People*, *Glamour*, the *New York Times*, and *Variety* all published articles about Lentz, the world got a front-row seat in the theater of his unmasking. More bad news for the church—and when news like this breaks, so does some people's trust in the church.

The people who are affected by hypocrisy deserve a response when their trust is shattered. But what can we possibly convey to those who have been disillusioned by the church? Here are some thoughts:

1. *Hypocrisy must be met by acknowledging the problem for what it is.* This is our opportunity to concede the truth, to show humility, and to refrain from jumping on the defensive. It's here that we must validate the critics' concerns. The importance of validation—that is, acknowledging that the other person's emotions and experiences are meaningful— has been underscored by neuroscience.[1] Studies have shown that people cannot fully heal without validation. That's why it is so important to listen to, corroborate, and express remorse to people who have been wounded by hypocrisy. We've all seen relationships remain stuck because one person was unable or unwilling to validate the other person's pain. When we attempt to justify the unjustifiable, we paralyze relational progress. Acknowledging the hypocrisy should be a simple and obvious first step.

2. *We can remind the disillusioned that Jesus reserved his sharpest criticism for hypocrites.* We catch a glimpse of Jesus' disdain for hypocrisy in his interactions with the Pharisees and scribes: "Isaiah was right when he prophesied about you hypocrites; as it is written: 'These people honor me with their lips, but their hearts are far from me.'"[2] With one zinger, he unmasked their religious duplicity.

3. *We can't allow bad examples to negate the influence of good examples.* Before we get tied up in knots about some people's hypocrisy, we would do well to remind ourselves

of the abundant examples of integrity in church history, such as Polycarp, Susanna Wesley, D. L. Moody, William Wilberforce, Billy Graham, Joni Eareckson Tada, and many, many others. It would be unfair and shortsighted to discredit the full package of Christianity based on the examples of hypocrites, especially considering the testimony of exemplary Christians throughout the centuries whose lives were on splendid display for Christ.

Nevertheless, we must address the underlying question: Does hypocrisy in the church discredit the truth of Christianity? Simple answer: Not in the least. A person's failure to live up to the standards of their belief system doesn't undermine the entire system; it simply shows that the person has fallen short of whatever ideal they set for themselves.

The moral standards for Christians are revealed in Scripture for all to see. And it seems as if there are many people who are ready to pounce on us the moment we come up short. Not that we want to play gotcha, but it's not quite as easy to call out people with other beliefs—such as atheism—where there are no objective standards of right and wrong.

Just as you'll find scandals wherever you find humans, you'll also find hypocrisy. But what we're aiming to discern is whether the *standards* on which people build their lives are true and valid. Rejecting Christianity because some Christians are hypocrites would be like not buying a certain brand of shoes because the only people you've ever seen wearing them were troublemakers. It would be silly to reject the brand because of your limited observations of people who wear them.

If anything, the concern about hypocrisy among Christians points to a standard—a high and holy standard we all have broken.

This standard exists apart from us and is grounded in God's good and holy nature. God's moral commands flow from his character; and the more we keep his standards, the more we become like him. Even when we fall short, we can get back up and keep going.

Now let's consider, as we did in the previous chapter, how the contention of Christian hypocrisy shapes up in argument form, so we can either prove it or detect the fallacy. The argument could be framed as follows:

Premise 1: If there are hypocrites in the church, then Christianity is false.
Premise 2: There are hypocrites in the church.
Conclusion: Therefore, Christianity is false.

The problem with this argument is easy to detect. The truth of Christianity rises and falls on the resurrection of Jesus Christ, not on whether his followers have completely and faithfully upheld his standards. Examining a person's hypocrisy is not enough to invalidate his or her beliefs. We must look at the beliefs themselves.

What makes Christianity unique is that it recognizes the problem of hypocrisy, that humans are morally disadvantaged, and it points us to Jesus, who never suffered from hypocrisy, and reveals him as the only one suited to address the sin behind our hypocrisy—which he did by offering his life as a substitute on our behalf. Therefore, Christianity both recognizes the problem of hypocrisy and offers the solution to it. When we as Christians fall into hypocrisy, we don't invalidate Christianity; if anything, we reveal through our actions that we're broken and we need Jesus.

7

WHY DON'T CHURCHES HOLD THEIR LEADERS ACCOUNTABLE?

The world is threatened more by those who tolerate or encourage evil than by the evildoers themselves.

ALBERT EINSTEIN

In a September 2019 article released by *Politico*, Brandon Ambrosino begins a massive exposé with these words: "At Liberty University, all anyone can talk about is Jerry Falwell Jr. Just not in public." A trusted advisor to Falwell told Ambrosino, "When he does stupid stuff, people will mention it to others they consider confidants and not keep it *totally* secret. But they won't rat him out."[1] Less than a year later, all of that changed when Falwell resigned as president of the university as scandals surfaced in the tabloids revealing the cover-up of a nearly seven-year affair between Falwell's wife, Becki, and a hotel pool attendant named Giancarlo Granda.

In the days leading up to his resignation, Falwell posted an Instagram photo of himself aboard a yacht, with his belly sticking out and his pants unzipped, holding a drink in one hand and his other arm wrapped around the side of a pregnant Liberty employee. In the wake of his precipitous fall, the world watched as another so-called Christian leader was exposed for his hypocrisy. But, as Ambrosino's article made clear, Falwell's shady character was already obvious to those on the inside at Liberty University.

It's no wonder some people ask how churches—or, in this case, a Christian university—can ignore, cover up, or make excuses for hypocritical leaders. Why would they protect hypocrites instead of exposing them? The following are some reasons they often do:

1. *Sometimes churches or other Christian organizations fear their leaders' influence or power.* Because leaders often have the ability to manipulate, control, and intimidate their followers, they can use fear to buy silence. This was certainly the case at Liberty University, where Jerry Falwell Jr. led from a place of sheer power, and those who served near him chose to keep their mouths shut—and keep their jobs—rather than expose him.

2. *Sometimes people close to the leader don't recognize the hypocrisy and fail to believe the rumors.* This was certainly the case with Ravi Zacharias. The initial allegations baffled many people and caused a lot of Christians to initially come to his defense. I can still hear the absolute confusion in the voice of a dear friend who told me he had invited Zacharias to speak at his church, and that he couldn't comprehend how a person so seemingly Spirit-filled could have lived a double life. Like many, he was at a loss for how to interpret his experience in the aftermath of Ravi's death.

I don't blame him. I felt the same way. Zacharias had

projected such a kind, humble, above-reproach kind of character that many people were left dumbfounded when the evidence exposed him as a fraud. This underscores the problem, common in Christian circles, of putting too much stock in any one person. When we put someone on a pedestal and he or she falls, we're often left disillusioned. Another problem is the creation of leadership structures that make it easy for a corrupt leader to fly under the radar for so many years.

Atheist blogger Steve Baughman, who was rightfully bothered by Ravi Zacharias's unaddressed hypocrisy, said, "We need to have some systemic reflection and look at what are the structures that enabled a narcissistic abuser to fool so many people. . . . It took an evangelical village to enable him for decades, and that's the real lesson here. It's not about Ravi anymore. It's about the system that let him get away with this."[2] In the aftermath of the scandal, Ravi Zacharias International Ministries made a bad situation even worse by trying to defend their leader—going so far as to blame Ravi's accusers of trying to destroy his ministry. They later apologized and recognized the harm caused by making excuses for Zacharias. But above all, it was Zacharias's false image that led so many to initially grant him the benefit of the doubt.

3. *Sometimes ministries fear what it will mean for their organization if the truth comes out.* It could mean a public scandal, a loss of attendance, a reduction in giving, or even the loss of a job. But Christian organizations are not the only ones open to scrutiny here. The tables could also be turned on companies, political parties, and other religious institutions

that have been guilty of covering the truth to keep it from hurting their organizations. But that doesn't make it right.

4. *Sometimes churches are passive and fail to see that account-ability is a key responsibility—even when it feels unloving.* To say that it's unloving to hold someone accountable for their actions is a faulty view of love. This posture is unbiblical and flies in the face of sound biblical advice that exhorts us to speak the truth in love.[3] When a leader crosses a moral line, it is our obligation to speak the truth in love, whatever the cost.

5. *Sometimes Christians feel as if they are betraying their leaders if they confront their misdeeds.* This is especially true when a leader has been good to the flock or when staff members feel a sense of unrealistic loyalty to the leader. The burden of carrying a failed leader's secrets is not a cross that Christ expects us to bear. Rather, we owe it to God, to the church, *and* to the leader not to make excuses for the leader's hypo-critical behavior.

6. *Sometimes churches become so relationally attached to their leaders that they lose objectivity and fail to address problems for fear of losing that relationship.* People can feel torn between their allegiance to the person who has been exposed and their duty to rightfully confront the leader's moral failure. When the relational bonds are tight, it can be tempting to look the other way or rationalize questionable behavior. This can be especially true when there are family ties. God, however, does not look favorably on the ignoring of sin. A clear example of this can be seen in the lives of Eli and his two sons, Hophni and Phinehas, who served as priests

in Israel. At some point, Eli's sons lost their moral way, holding their religious posts with contempt, even to the point of taking the best of people's offerings for themselves and sleeping with the women who served at the entrance to the tent of meeting. Shockingly, even though Eli knew what was happening and rebuked his sons verbally, he did nothing to stop their behavior. Eventually, God intervened, chastised Eli for excusing his sons' wicked behavior, and brought about consequences that ultimately cost all three men their lives.[4] Passivity in the face of wrongdoing always comes with a price tag.

7. *Sometimes corrupt leaders are insulated by unhealthy structures that make it more difficult for others to act.* Some leaders create a cocoon to insulate themselves from accountability. Often, these leaders are heavy-handed, top-down, authoritarian types who lack vulnerability and shield themselves from influencers by creating layers of red tape to prevent access to them and their lives.

8. *Sometimes the people who could hold a leader accountable are engaged in their own sin, making them reluctant to initiate accountability.* In some churches, after years without any form of accountability, the church culture grows completely toxic. In situations like this, it isn't just a particular leader who needs to be confronted; the entire leadership structure needs to be called to account. This is an intimidating place for those in the congregation who are left to do the job—often in the absence of any real organizational power. All the power is in the hands of the corrupt leaders.

I heard a story about a Christian who challenged a

pastor living in habitual sin. When asked how he could continue to teach his congregation, the pastor said, "I've learned to not let it bother me, and I just keep preaching." That's what you call hypocritical leadership. And the reason he was able to get away with his habitual sin was that he was surrounded by other corrupt leaders who weren't about to hold him accountable.

9. *Sometimes leaders aren't held accountable because the people around them believe it's God's place, not theirs, to confront the wrongdoing.* While every fallen leader is ultimately responsible before God, that doesn't mean he or she isn't also accountable to others. No one gets a free pass; every leader is called to a high standard and should humbly welcome accountability to guard against moral failure.

This list is far from exhaustive, but it touches on some of the main reasons why certain churches and other Christian organizations may not hold their leaders accountable. The next time you feel tempted to excuse a leader's immoral behavior, here is some timely advice you can follow:

1. *Acknowledge the behavior.* Don't make or accept excuses. Refuse to be deceived; acknowledge there's a problem that must be addressed. Whatever consequences may come— for the leader or the organization—you must refuse to sweep problems under the rug and look the other way.

2. *Follow biblical protocol to address the behavior.* Churches may make excuses for hypocrisy, but the Bible doesn't. Paul's advice to Timothy remains helpful in terms of how to address allegations of wrongdoing by a leader: "Do not

entertain an accusation against an elder unless it is brought by two or three witnesses."[5] Paul was all too familiar with rabble-rousers who might try to run down a leader's character. For that reason, he directed Timothy to look for corroboration from multiple people.

Granted, some accusations will be so indicting, and the stakes too high, not to vet the person's claims. Paul also advised Timothy that if there were ample evidence of immoral behavior, he should confront it publicly, so that others who were tempted to such behavior would be duly warned and would think twice before acting out: "Those elders who are sinning you are to reprove before everyone, so that the others may take warning."[6]

Similarly, Jesus gave wise counsel for addressing immorality: "If your brother or sister sins, go and point out their fault, just between the two of you. If they listen to you, you have won them over. But if they will not listen, take one or two others along, so that 'every matter may be established by the testimony of two or three witnesses.' If they still refuse to listen, tell it to the church; and if they refuse to listen even to the church, treat them as you would a pagan or a tax collector."[7] Jesus went so far as to say that if the person shunned the rebukes, they were to be treated as a nonbeliever. Let that sink in. That's a powerful indictment, clearly indicating that believers should acknowledge their wrongdoing when it is revealed.

3. *Don't assume that God will excuse the hypocrisy.* It's no secret that God's reputation precedes him. Judgment is a running theme throughout Scripture. As we conclude this chapter, we must concede that the church all too often has been

far too passive in making excuses for hypocritical leaders. But even as wrong as these excuses are, they don't in any way support the claim that Christianity is false. Instead, when churches make excuses for hypocritical leaders, they reveal their failure to live in accordance with the Christian faith. We cannot use the fact that some Christians ignore hypocrisy in their leaders as an excuse to implicate God or Christianity. That, too, is a form of passivity that God will judge as sin.

As wrong as it is for churches to fail to address immoral behavior among their leadership, their failure doesn't prove that Christianity is false, any more than holding their leaders accountable would prove that the message and claims of Christianity are true. The veracity of the Christian faith rests on greater evidence than a leader's accountability.

SECTION 2

THE CHURCH IS NONACCEPTING

8

WHY DO CHRISTIANS USE GOD'S NAME TO OPPRESS OTHERS?

The number one cause of atheism is Christians. Those who proclaim God with their mouths and deny him with their lifestyles are what an unbelieving world finds simply unbelievable.

KARL RAHNER

Several years ago, on a trip to Bellingham, Washington, to teach a course for Logos Bible Software, I encountered one of those stereotypical street preachers who leverages God's good name to tell people how much God hates them, while yelling and warning passersby of God's coming judgment and the fires of hell that await them unless they repent. I couldn't help myself and tried to strike up a conversation with the man, but my efforts weren't warmly received—as you might imagine. When I questioned his methods, he informed me that I, too, was lost and needed to repent, lest hell's inferno soon welcome me. Comforting.

In my flesh, I felt like giving the guy an old-fashioned round-house, but that wouldn't have been helpful—nor would it have been loving—so I resisted. But here's what I can tell you. I and everyone else around me felt oppressed by this so-called Christian evangelist.

Unfortunately, there are overly zealous people out there who oppress others in the name of Christianity—though thankfully it's not the norm. Sadly, people like that often leave a bad taste in the mouths of nonbelievers, giving them one more reason to criticize Christianity. However, people who spew hatred and judgment in the name of Christianity should never be held up as the measure for authentic Christian faith; rather, they are the antithesis of it.

Critics of Christianity often point out the ways in which Christians have oppressed others through the ages: the Crusades; the Spanish Inquisition; the Salem witch trials; the slave trade; or, in our own day, the denigration of women, African Americans, or the LGBTQ community. Though no Christian with the slightest awareness of church history could deny that the church has seen its share of oppressors throughout the ages, neither can we fail to acknowledge the abundance of good done in the name of Jesus.

Consider the following brief examples: The first orphanages were run by churches. Various churches and individual Christians founded many of the great American universities, such as Harvard, Princeton, and Yale, to ensure that people would be given a proper education. The church was pivotal in leading society to abolish slavery, with leaders such as the British parliamentarian William Wilberforce. George Williams founded the YMCA to protect youth from the hazardous conditions on the streets. Likewise, William Booth founded the Salvation Army to care for the poor and disadvantaged. In our day, Millard and Linda Fuller started Habitat for Humanity to provide housing for the poor on an international level.

Today, churches everywhere strive to help the homeless, offer protection and alternatives to women considering abortion, work to eradicate the sex trade preying on young women and girls, and feed the hungry . . . and that's just scratching the surface of the good done in the name of Jesus. Far from oppressing the world, many contemporary Christians seek to free the world from oppression in various ways.

So, why has the modern church been so regularly accused of oppression? Here's why. Our culture has become so fragile and intolerant of opposing viewpoints that many people feel oppressed if we simply disagree with their moral decisions. Never mind that differing viewpoints are part and parcel of a free society. Today we are reaping the bitter fruit of thinkers such as Friedrich Nietzsche, Sigmund Freud, and Karl Marx, all of whom believed that religious morality was an oppressive delusion.

Nietzsche famously pronounced that "God is dead." His allegation wasn't so much that God had died, but rather that he had become irrelevant, and that we "no longer need Christianity as a guarantee of morality."[1] What is needed, according to this philosophy, is a master morality of the strong-willed who can break free from the religious shackles of the past. The herd morality of the masses limits human flourishing and is meant to be resisted in order to discover one's own way.

Freud viewed religion as a psychological crutch, the outgrowth of a desire rooted in "wish fulfilment" that ultimately suffocates its victims with oppressive guilt. For Marx, "Religion is the sigh of the oppressed creature. . . . It is the opium of the people."[2]

These thinkers believed that the moral framework imposed on humanity by the religious class needed to be set aside for human fulfillment to come to fruition. And we see evidence of such thinking in our culture today. Nietzsche, Freud, Marx, and others heavily influenced the postmodern mindset; their ideas have been coupled with various schools of critical theory that view everything through the lens of an oppressed/oppressor framework. Individual expression, elimination of sexual oppression, being authentic and true to oneself, casting off all forms of hierarchy—these are the emerging values of our culture. But this new morality fails to recognize its ethical weaknesses.

Here's what I think is oppressive: being forced to agree with people who are offended by beliefs that don't square with their own. With many people unwilling or unable to stomach competing opinions, America has become a cancel culture. Instead of allowing alternative opinions a seat at the table of ideas, some people would rather force others into submission by means of public ridicule or condemnation. We've all witnessed this sort of oppression—from demands that all white people "repent" of their racism, to people who go ballistic if anyone uses the "wrong" pronoun, to LGBTQ activists deriding anyone who doesn't celebrate gay pride.

It has been said many times that "ideas have consequences," and some greater than others. The ideas of such thinkers as Nietzsche, Freud, and Marx—and we could certainly add others, including Darwin, Foucault, and Derrida—have heavily influenced our contemporary culture. Sadly, many people who are driven by these ideas don't seem to realize it. They are fueled by a passion often bereft of knowledge about the philosophical engine that keeps their movements moving.

Bottom line: I don't buy the proposition that Christianity, at its heart, is oppressive. Christianity promotes a morality that some find constraining, but it doesn't write people off and demonize those who don't ascribe to faith in Jesus. Rather, it could well be argued that the oppressors are those who want to force Christians and other religious believers into moral straitjackets.

The incursion of cancel culture into our society has created a complete mess. It's as if we've hit an iceberg, and the great ship called America is now sinking to the bottom of the sea. Ours is no longer a nation where we can agree to disagree about our beliefs and opinions and yet still unite, sharing nonpartisan or bipartisan agreement on policies. No, a new crowd has emerged that is more than ready to punish, ridicule, cancel, and run off anyone who doesn't fall in line with the program—whatever that program might be. Again, that's oppressive. In the next five chapters, we will examine various accusations of oppression levied at the church today—in the areas of homosexuality, gender, race, women, and pro-life issues.

9

AREN'T MOST CHRISTIANS HOMOPHOBIC?

It's almost as if the Bible was written by racist, sexist, homophobic, violent, sexually frustrated men, instead of a loving God. Weird.

RICKY GERVAIS

Back in high school, my buddies and I cruised over to Santa Cruz to enjoy a day in the sun, beach style. According to custom, we smoked a bunch of marijuana, and I got so high that I passed out on the sand. When I came back around, I was met with hysterical laughter. I couldn't figure out what was so funny . . . until I learned that one of my buddies had taken suntan oil and written "I'm gay" on my back. By the time I woke up—severely sunburned after several hours of exposure—the words were glowing large for all to see as I walked along the beach.

When I think about my high school days, I'd be lying if I said that my friends and I were kind in our attitudes toward gay people. Aversion to same-gender attraction was a common sentiment back then. On top of that, I lived an hour south of San Francisco, with its thriving gay community, at a time of heightened sensitivity due to the newly identified HIV virus, which was thought to especially affect the gay community. I lost a cousin to AIDS, and seeing him waste away was a lot for me to comprehend at the time. It was certainly no joke.

Obviously, much has changed in our culture since then, and it hurts my heart to imagine what it must have been like for people in the LGBTQ community to feel isolated, rejected, and mocked by so many in society. Regardless of what one thinks about same-sex attraction, gay people should never be treated as outcasts. People are people, and we all need to feel loved.

And yet, when I think about *how* our culture has changed, it seems as if the script has been flipped from exclusion to celebration. Now it seems as if anyone who doesn't support "gay pride" is mocked or dismissed as "homophobic." But this is little more than a bully tactic to pressure people into conformity.

The word *homophobic* refers to someone who has an *irrational fear* of gay people. But just because someone disapproves of the gay lifestyle doesn't mean he or she is homophobic. We wouldn't say that someone who believes people should wait until they're married to have sex has a *phobia* about anyone who has sex outside of marriage. And neither should we assume that anyone who disapproves of LGBTQ sexuality is homophobic.

Growing up in the San Francisco Bay Area, one of the more liberal places in the nation, I was a poster child for a liberal lifestyle. I was sexually promiscuous, pro-choice, pro-drugs—you name it, I supported it. But everyone I knew—as far as I knew—did not understand same-sex attraction. And most people in the LGBTQ community kept their sexual preferences under wraps. I cannot think of one openly gay person at my high school. That's amazing, considering where I lived and how large my high school was.

As far as the view that all Christians are homophobic, it was my becoming a Christian that helped me *not* to mistreat same-sex-attracted people. Christianity taught me that every person is valued and loved by God as his unique image-bearers. I can assure you that is not a value I grew up with in the California public school system. That is a distinctly Christian value. The truth is, I knew a lot more homophobic people as a non-Christian than I ever have as a Christian. And after three decades as a Christian, I can't think of a single Christian I've known personally who wouldn't whole-heartedly agree that we need to treat the LGBTQ community with love. If anything, the church at large has sometimes gone too far in accepting the LGBTQ ideology, so much so that some have forsaken the clear teaching of the Bible to ensure that gay people feel accepted. If Christians believe the lie that not affirming every sexual preference means they are unloving and homophobic, it's no wonder so many have raised the rainbow flag.

So why don't more churches celebrate the LGBTQ lifestyle? The answer is simple. In the Bible, they don't see God celebrating, or even condoning, homosexuality. There isn't a single passage of Scripture that casts a favorable light on same-sex attraction, much less gay marriage. Neither is there anything in Scripture that paints sex outside of marriage in a positive light. The Bible is clear that sex is intended for a husband and wife in the context of marriage, for the dual purpose of pleasure and procreation. Christians who don't endorse same-sex attraction are trying to remain faithful to their understanding of the Bible. In other words, it's a matter of conscience.

During the 2022 baseball season, several players for the Tampa Bay Rays opted not to wear an LGBTQ logo on their uniforms to celebrate Gay Pride Month. Predictably, they were criticized and reviled online and through social media. Bullying people into affirming or celebrating something that goes against their conscience simply to fit the societal mold is both unloving and intolerant. But ours is a time in which corporations, schools, government officials, and even sports teams are rallying in support of Gay Pride Month, and if anyone fails to join the party, there are many people who are ready to expose, cancel, and humiliate them.

Many Christians are willing to value people in the LGBTQ community and even shower them with love, but they can't deny their own conscience at the expense of celebrating what is clearly forbidden by God. After all, it isn't Christians that our culture needs to fear; it's people in our culture who won't leave room for differing viewpoints, who turn to oppressive measures to force others into compliance. Consequently, at the risk of being labeled as homophobic, Christians must lovingly refuse to bow to cultural pressure to affirm what the Bible condemns. The way forward won't be easy, but it would be a lot easier if everyone would allow some room for people to be true to their own conscience.

10

DOES GOD REALLY CARE ABOUT MY GENDER IDENTITY?

Traditionally, if a man *felt* like a woman yet *inhabited* a male body, his feelings, not his body, were viewed as the problem. They were considered something to be resisted, modified if possible, and contrary to what *was*. Currently, what one *is* is being determined by what one *feels*—an ominous trend when one considers its implications. It is, in essence, an attempt to define reality by desire, knowledge by intuition.

JOE DALLAS

Being in ministry provides leaders with a front-row seat to the good, the bad, and the ugly of people's lives. If I've learned anything through the years, it's this: *Life is messy*. And it doesn't come with a nicely packaged answer to suit every occasion. Consequently, ministry requires relational finesse, the ability to empathize, and a willingness to tactfully engage with emotionally difficult situations. Often, ministry is marked by trial and error. Two steps forward, one step back.

Here's something else I've learned: *Ministry is hard*. It's hard because people go through difficult times that will break your heart. I know what it's like to walk with families through horrendous loss. I've officiated at funerals resulting from drug overdoses, suicides, and tragic car accidents. And that barely scratches the surface of the shattered lives into which I've been invited through hardship.

One of the most difficult issues confronting the church today is helping people navigate the complexities of their sexuality, especially when it includes gender dysphoria—the feeling of being trapped inside a wrong-gendered body. I witnessed the pain of this firsthand over lunch one day with a man whose son had recently undergone sex-reassignment surgery and would be coming home to visit in a few days. The father was having a hard time processing how he would react when he picked up his transgendered child at the airport.

Over my years in ministry, I've learned that empathy goes a long way in difficult situations such as this. There are no easy answers, and my heart genuinely went out to both parties. It was easy for me to understand how challenging it was for the father to watch his son reject his male identity and insist that the parents now treat him as their daughter. Nothing could erase their love for their child, but neither did it remove the relational awkwardness they all now had to navigate.

Had I been talking to the son, I easily could have empathized with how brutal it must be to feel trapped inside the wrong body. I would not make light of the mental and emotional torture he had certainly been experiencing. Compassion was my primary emotion for everyone concerned.

If empathy doesn't come naturally to you, just try to imagine what it would be like to look at yourself in the mirror and yet feel emotionally and mentally like a member of the opposite sex. That would be torturous, right? It's no wonder that many in the trans community have felt such despair. Now imagine the fear of being rejected by those you love the most if you decide to move forward with sex reassignment. It doesn't take much of a heart to break over how difficult this would be. In this instance, both the father and the son acknowledged the difficulty and at least tried to put themselves in the other's shoes. But that's a lot to process.

Validation and empathy are among the more positive capabilities of our being human. Call it exercising good people skills. But validation and empathy don't equate to agreeing with someone else's moral stance on a position that runs contrary to Scripture. Nowhere does the Bible advise us to compromise our beliefs in order to validate someone else's. That said, here are a few points to remember about gender dysphoria and sex reassignment:

1. *Feeling like a particular gender doesn't make a person that gender.* The fact is, there's no such thing as a *true* sex change. Sex reassignment doesn't change a person's chromosomes. Gender is a fixed biological reality at the most basic level of our being. It's not something we figure out along life's journey.

   In 2018, news broke about Oli London, a Caucasian male from England, who reportedly spent more than $100,000 for multiple plastic surgeries to make him look like the K-pop star Jimin from the Korean boy band BTS. From there he moved on to identifying as a Korean woman, modeling himself after Rosé from the girl band Blackpink. Then, in November 2022, London announced he was returning to his biological sex—that of a male, though he still refers to himself as Korean—and expressing relief that he had not gone ahead with reassignment surgery, which he realized he would have regretted.[1] Interestingly, London attributed his decision to return to his male identity to Christianity, saying, "Letting Jesus and God into my heart

[has] saved my life. It's brought me back to who I am as a person, finding God."[2] So there's hope.

Some trans advocates might argue that Oli London is an outlier and not a good example because he obviously changed his mind and didn't get the surgery. But I have to ask, what if he had gotten reassignment surgery and then changed his mind again? He would be filled with regret and have no way of fixing his mistake. This happens more often than you might think.

There was a time, not too long ago, when people suffering from gender dysphoria were told that their *feelings* were the problem; now they're being told their *physique* is the issue. And here's the irony in our culture: On the one hand, there are people who say that gender is a fluid social construct, based on societal norms, not on biology. On the other hand, people are still choosing gender reassignment surgery to change their appearance. If biology is nondeterminative for gender, why undergo reassignment surgery?

2. *Our identity is rooted in God, the author of our gender.* God is the one who assigns gender, not we ourselves. The text of Genesis 1:27 is pretty straightforward: "God created mankind in his own image, in the image of God he created them; male and female he created them." That's saying something. The Bible contains 1,189 chapters, and we learn this lesson right away in chapter 1. If God created us as male or female and we seek to deny or reverse this, we are essentially rejecting the identity he has given us. The challenges for those struggling with their gender identity are real, but tinkering with one's gender is not the answer. Our identity encompasses so much more than gender preference.

Because our identity is rooted in God, in whose image we are created, it is not reducible to our sexual preferences. As God's image bearers, who are created as either male or female, we are *also* created as moral, rational, emotional, and volitional beings. We have a much broader identity to offer the world than just our sexuality. But that's where our culture seems to have become fixated. People are being led to believe that sexuality is the key to understanding our humanity. So it's no wonder that some people are demanding that we accept their gender preference at all costs.

But that's the lie we want to expose. Our identity as human beings is so much more than our sexuality. So much bigger. So much more detailed. We're sexual beings, yes, but not merely sexual beings. The Bible doesn't directly address the issues of gender dysphoria and sex reassignment. But what it does say is that we are fearfully and wonderfully made in the image of God, and we are born either male or female.[3]

There is much more that could be said on the topic, and we all must be prepared to engage in this conversation at some point without capitulating to the culture. In the meantime, we can validate as meaningful the emotions and experiences of gender-dysphoric people, demonstrate empathy toward them, and remind them of the truth that they were created by a loving God.

Though gender dysphoria can certainly have moral implications, as Christians, we must realize that simply questioning one's gender doesn't mean that someone is rebelling against God or trying to be sinful. Many people, especially young Gen Zers, are confused because of the social messaging they have received. We can hope and pray that our churches will become safe spaces for people who are dealing with gender dysphoria—by listening, validating, praying for, comforting, and redirecting those who are grappling with identity issues, all in an atmosphere of love, grace, acceptance, and truth.

11

WHY ARE SO MANY CHRISTIANS RACISTS?

I refuse to accept the view that mankind is so tragically bound to the starless midnight of racism and war that the bright daybreak of peace and brotherhood can never become a reality. . . . I believe that unarmed truth and unconditional love will have the final word in reality.

DR. MARTIN LUTHER KING JR.

On May 25, 2020, onlookers watched in horror as Minneapolis police officer Derek Chauvin knelt on George Floyd's back and neck for nine and a half minutes while arresting him on suspicion of passing a counterfeit twenty-dollar bill. The arrest ultimately led to Floyd's tragic death as he managed to rasp his final words: "I can't breathe." Protests soon spread like wildfire across the nation as people demanded justice for Floyd. And when all was said and done, Chauvin was found guilty as charged and sentenced to more than twenty-two years in prison.

In the aftermath of Floyd's death, I called my good friend Bryan Loritts, a well-known African American pastor. I knew that George Floyd's death was an especially sensitive topic, but even so, I wasn't prepared for what Bryan would say to me. When I asked how he was doing, he floored me with his response: "Bobby, when I first saw what happened to Floyd, I was tempted to write off all white people. But then I saw your face and remembered that all white people aren't that way."

Talk about a humbling moment of friendship. I was completely caught off guard. But in that sacred relational space, I realized more than ever the importance of cross-cultural connection in the body of Christ. Bryan has dedicated much of his life and ministry to fostering racial reconciliation, and he was vulnerable enough with me to underscore how vital it is to have diversified relationships, especially during challenging times.

As a white man, I am ashamed of our nation's racial sins. It's mind-boggling to realize that for much of our country's history, African Americans were deemed less than human; not permitted to vote; not permitted to use the same restrooms or drink from the same water fountains as their white counterparts; not allowed to attend the same schools or sit in the same sections at public events or in some churches. And, sadly, at times in our history, some professing Christians have misquoted or misappropriated Scripture to defend everything from slavery to segregation. This is wrong and is a perversion of what the Bible says about how people should get along and be treated. American history is undeniably checkered when it comes to race, and there's still much work to be done. Though we'll never do it perfectly, that shouldn't stop us from trying to make things better.

Some people have argued that Christianity is a racist religion, or a white man's religion, but that claim doesn't hold up to scrutiny— especially when you consider that the earliest Christian communities were composed primarily of Near Easterners and North Africans. Unfortunately, modern artistic depictions of Jesus as a brown-haired, blue-eyed Savior haven't helped dispel this rumor, but scholars have long agreed that, as a first-century Palestinian Jew, Jesus was most certainly a person of color. Christianity is neither a white man's religion nor a racist religion.

Though Christianity is clearly *not* a racist religion, that doesn't mean that some who profess to be Christians aren't, or haven't been, racist. But how can that be?

Several factors contribute to someone becoming a racist—with sin, of course, at the top of the list. Despite the Christian ethos of equality, people always find ways to feel superior toward others. For some who have grown up in a racially toxic environment, it may be an ongoing struggle to shed their ingrained racial biases. Others may have had an unfortunate experience that has made it hard for them to overcome their unfair prejudices toward a particular group. For others, their racist attitudes are rooted in a lack of exposure or interaction across racial lines. It's easy to retain skewed ideas when you stay inside a socially isolated bubble. And, of course, how the media portray people of different races generally doesn't help to break down barriers. Whatever one's motives might be, one thing we can say for certain: When Christians harbor racist attitudes or foster racist behavior, they are acting contrary to Scripture. The following four points highlight the biblical, Christian perspective on diversity:

1. *Christianity recognizes different ethnicities, but only one human race.* When the apostle Paul addressed the crowd on the Areopagus in Athens, he declared that God "made from one man every nation of mankind to live on all the face of the earth."[1] We humans all descended from God's original first pair, Adam and Eve.

2. *All people are created equal in God's image, regardless of skin color, ethnicity, or any other factor.* In the very first chapter

of the Bible, we read, "God created mankind in his own image, in the image of God he created them; male and female he created them."[2] The idea that humans were created in God's image is repeated throughout Scripture. Here are two examples worth noting:

Whoever sheds human blood, by humans shall their blood be shed; for in the image of God has God made mankind.[3]

Here we see that murder is considered a capital crime because it devalues the life of another person created in the image of God.

With the tongue we praise our Lord and Father, and with it we curse human beings, who have been made in God's likeness. . . . My brothers and sisters, this should not be.[4]

This is a powerful reminder that minimizing people with our words is an affront to our Creator, who made people in his own image. From these two verses alone, we can deduce that all people are equally valuable to God and that no one should be harmed physically, verbally, or emotionally. Unlike other worldviews, biblical Christianity offers us the theological motivation to properly value the worth and dignity of others by esteeming people made in the image of God through our actions and words. Perhaps this is why non-Christians are baffled when they witness racism in the life of a professed believer in Jesus.

3. *According to the Bible, racism is not a skin issue; it's a sin issue.* The problem is not the color of someone's skin but the corruption of our hearts. Consider the story of Peter in

Acts 10. He was praying on a rooftop when God gave him a vision instructing him to take the gospel to the Gentiles, people whom the Jews considered unclean. Peter was called to expand his comfort zone and to "not call anything impure that God has made clean."[5]

Sadly, sometimes change is short-lived, and Peter later needed a stern reminder that the gospel is for everyone and that Jewish favoritism was unacceptable in the eyes of God. He met his match in Paul, who called him out in Antioch for failing to engage with the Gentiles there.[6] Peter had slipped back into his old ways of favoring his own people and shunning non-Jews. Unfortunately, the roots of prejudice can be hard to pull up. But it's our responsibility as Christians to confront racism wherever we see it among us.

4. *Racism is contrary to the all-inclusive message of the gospel.* According to Scripture, God is no respecter of persons. Writing to the Galatians, Paul clears away all distinctions, including those involving ethnicity: "There is neither Jew nor Gentile, neither slave nor free, nor is there male and female, for you are all one in Christ Jesus."[7] The message is for everyone. That's the good news of which Jesus reminds us: "For God so loved the world that he gave his one and only Son, that *whoever* believes in him shall not perish but have eternal life."[8]

Not only is Christianity not racist, but it is our *solution* to racism. Christianity is for everyone. Through the gospel message, we learn the secret of being reconciled not only to God but to all people as well. The death of Jesus on the cross models for us in full color how to forgive, love, offer grace, show mercy, and live as one. The world needs the church to take up the cross of Christ, and through the radical transforming relational principles of forgiveness, love, grace, and mercy, we can demonstrate that Christianity holds the key to eliminating racism and all other prejudice.

12

DOESN'T CHRISTIANITY DEVALUE WOMEN?

In my thirties, I started to explore the historical question of whether Christianity is good for women. The answer? A resounding "yes." This cuts against what most of my non-Christian friends believe. In their minds, Christianity is repressive and demeaning to women, and any differentiation of roles is anathema. But they don't realize that many of the things we take for granted when it comes to the value of women were given to us by Christianity.

REBECCA MCLAUGHLIN

Christianity doesn't devalue women, . . . but, sadly, some Christians do. I saw this firsthand in Bible college when we tackled the subject of biblical submission. As the professor unpacked the language, some of my male classmates were extra intentional about voicing their "amens." I remember being annoyed as they shouted, "Amen, brother. Preach it."

Though I had no issue with what the Bible says about submission, I did struggle with the condescending way in which those young men responded. It seemed degrading to the women in the class, and my heart went out to them. But despite the tendency of some men to disparage women, the Bible does not portray women as inferior to men.

Before we look at what the Bible *does* say, we would do well to reflect for a moment on how women were perceived in the prevailing culture. The contrast will quickly become clear between early Christianity and the cultural norms of the first century. It has been well established that the Greco-Roman world considered women second-class citizens. Grecian women were unable to vote or acquire their own land, and they certainly played less of a role than men in societal development. Under Roman law, women had no legal rights; in fact, they weren't even considered citizens.

In Israel as well, the culture during biblical times clearly devalued women. There was even a morning prayer in which Jewish men exclaimed, "God, thank you for not making me a woman." Talk about degrading. So, we would be foolish and historically ignorant to deny that abuses against women developed among the Jewish people, but that wasn't the result of following God's laws. Instead, it was a consequence of their assimilating the mores of surrounding cultures. From the earliest stages of their formation as a nation, the Israelites chased after foreign idols and took wives from outside the covenant community. As God's chosen people, they struggled long and hard with distinguishing themselves from the surrounding nations and consequently found themselves in captivity on more than one occasion.

There's no way around it. Women in the ancient world were often treated as the property of men, existing primarily to serve a man's needs, bear his children, and tend to the affairs of the household. It's no wonder women felt oppressed. But despite the common notion that Christianity is oppressive to women, the Bible tells a different story.

By the time Jesus began his public ministry, women were probably more than ready for his refreshing perspective. Far from belittling women, Jesus honored their inestimable worth as humans created in God's image. Think about his interactions with them.

He taught them, empowered them, healed them, saved them, and interacted freely with them, regardless of their sin, ethnicity, or ailments. He listened to women, praised women, and enjoyed the company of women, even including them as part of his ministry caravan. Even while on the cross, he ensured that his mother's needs would be cared for, and he permitted women to be the first eyewitnesses of his resurrection.[1]

This is not insignificant. In the ancient world, a woman's testimony was considered less reliable than a man's. So, if you were trying to fabricate a story about Jesus rising from the dead, in a culture where a woman's testimony was all but discounted, the last thing you would do is have women be the first eyewitnesses of the empty tomb. But the Gospel writers simply reported how the events occurred. Entrusting women as the first messengers of his resurrection shows the value Jesus placed on their testimony.

Women were drawn to Jesus precisely because he offered them a greater chance at a life of equal worth and dignity to their male counterparts.

Some might say, "Jesus isn't the problem, Bobby. Paul is." That's partly due to the translation of Paul's talk about submission, which certainly doesn't sit well with a lot of people today. Unfortunately, some men have used Paul's words to dominate women. It's the abuse of the term to which many people react—whether they realize it or not—not the original understanding that Paul intended.

Here's what Paul *doesn't* mean by the term. Submission doesn't mean women are less valuable than men, or that women aren't supposed to have a voice; neither does it mean that a woman must follow her husband *regardless* of his decisions or actions. Notice, too, that Paul begins his instructions for married couples by talking about *mutual* submission.[2]

Yes, Paul does say in the very next verse that a woman must

submit to her husband: "Wives, submit yourselves to your own husbands as you do to the Lord."[3] But continue reading to discover Paul's charge to men: "Husbands, love your wives, just as Christ loved the church and gave himself up for her."[4]

So, how exactly did Christ love the church? Well, he died for it. Whenever I teach this passage, I anticipate the objection to women submitting to their husbands by quickly reminding my audience that it's the men who are called to *lay down their lives* for their wives. So much for misogyny or lording it over women. If you're a woman who struggles with the idea of biblical submission, let me ask you a question: Would you rather *submit* or *die*? The husband is called to ultimate submission—to die, to lay down his life. And why would he do that? Because he loves his wife and recognizes her inestimable worth.

That said, equal worth doesn't mean we don't have different roles to play. And for some, that's the friction point. But male headship doesn't mean that men are more highly esteemed by God. No, it reflects the order of creation, and it means that men will be held more *accountable* by God. For the purpose of ordering society, God put in place a structure to help eliminate some of the confusion. That's not to say every household functions the same way. Not at all. It's just that the husband will have to answer to God for how well he executed his role as a servant leader in his home.

Roles aren't unique to the family. They're needed at every level of society for proper functioning. Even within the Trinity—one God revealed in three persons—there is role distinction. Each person is coequal with the other two, but each has a different role to play in God's redemptive plan for humanity. Jesus, during his time on earth, submitted to his Father's will, while at the same time making assertions such as, "I and the Father are one."[5] Thus we have an example of how men and women can be equal, yet have distinct roles.

Not everyone sees eye to eye when it comes to gender roles. *Complementarians* would argue that both sexes are created equal but they have different functional roles to play. *Hard complementarians* contend that roles are sharply distinguished between the sexes, whereas for *soft complementarians*, those roles may overlap. *Egalitarians* would agree that both sexes are created equal, but they go further than *soft complementarians* in saying that women are justified to serve in every way that men are—thus blurring role distinctions altogether.

Though Christians differ in their views on the role of women, the Bible never degrades the value of women by considering them inferior to men. Followers of the example set by Jesus both elevate and celebrate the value of women. Far from sexually objectifying women, as so many in our contemporary culture do, Jesus reminds us to treat women with the utmost respect, love, and dignity.

Men who are abusive to women are blatantly violating the clear teaching of Scripture. Sadly, the world is filled with oppressive men because the world is full of sinful men. And, of course, oppression doesn't happen solely in Christian circles. It happens wherever power is abused, whether by domineering businessmen, politicians, teachers, or religious leaders. Wherever you find people, you'll find one person oppressing another. But God calls us to a higher standard. He calls men to lay down their lives for their wives, families, and friends.[6]

The message of the Bible is that we are "*all* one in Christ." Christianity frees both men and women to discover their equal value through Christ alone.

13

WHY ARE CHRISTIANS SO OBSESSED WITH PRO-LIFE?

When pro-life advocates claim that elective abortion unjustly takes the life of a defenseless human being, they are not saying they dislike abortion. They are saying it's objectively wrong, regardless of how one feels about it.

SCOTT KLUSENDORF

There are two words I can still hear echoing from when I was seventeen years old: "I'm pregnant." I was sitting on the edge of my girlfriend's bed when she broke the news. After a moment of stunned silence, I managed to say, "I'll support you with whatever decision you want to make." A host of fears soon overwhelmed me. It was my senior year of high school, and I was young, irresponsible, and afraid to tell my parents, thinking, *They will surely disown me.*

Not long after the initial bombshell, while I was still absorbing the enormity of determining what we should do, my girlfriend informed me that she was going to get an abortion.

The day it happened was surreal. She felt more comfortable going with just her parents, so I went to school while they took her to Stanford Medical Center in Palo Alto to have the procedure. I remember walking around campus that day knowing deep down that something was morally dark about our decision, but I didn't see an alternative—or, at least, not a comfortable one.

I waited until school was out to head to her house, and the awkwardness of showing up there was palpable. She was resting on the pull-out coach in the family room, and I can still recall the extreme discomfort I felt around her parents—especially her dad—knowing I was culpable. My girlfriend and I were never the same after that tragic day. We continued to date in the years that followed, but we were both haunted by guilt. She met with a psychologist to process the pain of what had happened, and that might have been a good idea for me as well, though I never did.

It wasn't until I became a Christian that I was able to work through the guilt I harbored from that abortion. I remember, as a new believer, reading Psalm 139, and how it pierced my heart to reflect on the words:

> You created my inmost being;
>> you knit me together in my mother's womb.
> I praise you because I am fearfully and wonderfully made;
>> your works are wonderful,
>> I know that full well.
> My frame was not hidden from you
>> when I was made in the secret place,
>> when I was woven together in the depths of the earth.
> Your eyes saw my unformed body;
>> all the days ordained for me were written in your book
>> before one of them came to be.[1]

Now that I was a Christian, having already experienced the tragic truth of abortion, Psalm 139 was all it took to settle my position on the issue. Today, I am unashamedly pro-life. Deep down, I knew that abortion was wrong even before I became a Christian, but I still found a way to rationalize the decision.

We've heard all the reasons people give:

"Having a baby would dramatically change my life."
"I can't afford a baby right now."
"I don't want to be a single mother."
"I'm having relationship problems."
"I have completed my childbearing."
"I'm not ready for another child."
"I don't want people to know I had sex or got pregnant."
"I don't feel mature enough to raise a child."[2]

As Christians, we can find no way around the sanctity of human life. The Bible is clear that babies are a work of art being stitched together by God himself inside the womb. Even beyond Psalm 139, we find biblical support for the concept of personhood within the womb. For example, God told Jeremiah the prophet, "Before I formed *you* in the womb I knew *you*, before *you* were born I set *you* apart; I appointed *you* as a prophet to the nations."[3] The language is personal. Then there is King David, the author of Psalm 139, who also wrote, "Surely I was sinful at birth, sinful from the time my mother conceived *me*."[4] David refers to his unborn self as "me"—directly acknowledging his personhood within the womb.

Personhood within the womb was also clearly recognized under Mosaic law. If someone injured a pregnant woman, causing her to miscarry, it was considered a capital crime.[5] Of particular interest is the Hebrew word *yeled*, used to describe the unborn child in this passage. It is the same word used elsewhere to refer to young children.

In the New Testament, there is an interesting passage in which John the Baptist leaps in Elizabeth's womb when Mary, who is pregnant with Jesus, enters the room.[6] It is worth noting that the Greek word *brephos*, used to describe John the Baptist inside the womb in this passage, is the same word used to describe the infant Jesus in the manger.[7]

The Bible doesn't distinguish between a preterm baby and a baby who has been born. Either way, the child is considered a personal work of art from the moment of conception.[8] So, for Bible-believing Christians, the case is closed. The next time someone tries to tell you there's just a clump of tissue inside the womb, not a baby, don't forget the verses mentioned above. We are also fortunate to have cutting-edge technology, which supports our position. Have you seen the latest 3D ultrasound pictures? They're nothing short of amazing!

Another common pro-choice argument is that a woman has a right to control her own body, and normally I would agree. But if the unborn child is a *person*, as we've seen, there are now *two people* whose bodies we must consider. God has a purpose for every human life, and for that reason alone abortion is not an option for us as Christians. There have always been unwanted pregnancies and children born of rape or incest, and that will unfortunately always be the case. But those heartbreaking realities do not nullify the personhood of the unborn child. Our responsibility as the church is to treat everyone with love and compassion, including unborn children and women facing crisis pregnancies.

The church must do all it can to help women with unplanned pregnancies—both before and after the children are born. We must be there for these mothers with our care, resources, empathy, and prayers. But we cannot condone the taking of a child's life in the name of helping a woman in crisis due to pregnancy. That's not a biblical option for us.

I want to close with a word of encouragement for those who, like me, may find themselves trapped in their guilt due to an abortion from their past. If that's you, if you feel emotionally stuck, you need to know that the Bible offers a healing solution, based on the character and promises of God: "God is light; in him there is no darkness at all. . . . If we confess our sins, he is faithful and just and will forgive us our sins and purify us from all unrighteousness."[9]

If you have confessed your sin, and yet still feel guilty, meditate on Romans 8:1: "Therefore, there is now no condemnation for those who are in Christ Jesus." If you have confessed your sin and have sought forgiveness, *you're forgiven*. You are loved. And you have been bought with a price. Let those assurances replace your anguish with peace.

THE PROBLEMS OF EVIL AND SUFFERING

14

WHY DOES GOD ALLOW EVIL IN THE WORLD?

We do not know the reason God allows evil and suffering to continue, or why it is so random, but . . . it cannot be that he does not love us. It cannot be that he does not care. He is so committed to our ultimate happiness that he was willing to plunge into the greatest depths of suffering himself. He understands us, he has been there, and he assures us that he has a plan to eventually wipe away every tear.

TIMOTHY KELLER

There's a common argument out there that goes something like this: If God were truly all-powerful, he could get rid of all evil and suffering; and if God were really all-good, he *would* get rid of evil and suffering. Therefore, because evil and suffering still exist, God must not be all-powerful, or all-good, . . . or perhaps he's neither.

Scripture, however, reveals a God who is both omnipotent and omni-benevolent, and yet evil and suffering still exist. How might we reconcile this tension?

I have the privilege of cohosting a nationally syndicated radio show called *Pastors' Perspective*. One of the most frequent questions we get from callers is this: "Couldn't God have made us free without allowing evil?" On the surface, it sounds like an easy solution that would have prevented such a messy existence. But it's not that easy. It would require an unthinkable sacrifice from humanity for that kind of world to exist. Something would have to give, and that something is our *free will*. There is no logical way for God to have created us as free creatures without the *potential* for evil. The alternative would be for us to function as automatons. Without freedom of will, our obedience would be manipulated and meaningless. Our love for God, our moral obedience, and our desire to please him would be preprogrammed, and thereby pointless. Our personal autonomy would be nonexistent.

But God did not create us as automatons; he made us free creatures, giving us the best possible opportunity to thrive. But even though we were created by a perfect God and placed in a perfect environment, we rebelled in short order—and we've had a mess on our hands ever since. No, God didn't ask us whether we wanted to be created in the first place, nor whether we *wanted* to live according to the rules he established. But I'm not sure we know what we would be asking for in a world that was anything but free. Even given the choice, I'm not sure we would forfeit our free will to eliminate evil and suffering.

Imagine telling people that they could eliminate all evil and suffering from their lives, simply by surrendering their free will to God. Do you think they'd bite? The next time someone says to you, "How could a good God allow so much evil?" you can say, "In order for us humans to truly be free, there must remain at least the possibility that evil and suffering will result from the decisions we freely make."

But don't stop there. Follow up that statement with a question, as I did with a caller during a live radio show. Here's the question: "Which freedoms would you be willing to give up?" The freedom to act out sexually? The freedom to think what you want? The freedom to intoxicate yourself? The freedom to say what you want whenever you want? The freedom to go where you want to go? I suspect people would take their chances and stick with the free will option instead.

With some people, God simply can't win. They shake their fists at him for all the evil in the world, and yet they turn around and rail at him for curtailing their freedom. You can't have it both ways. But here's the silver lining: Even after our rebellion against him, God didn't just lock us up and throw away the key. He still wants to be in relationship with us, and he provided a way for that to happen. Moreover, he brought a measure of redemption out of the consequences of the Fall by revealing aspects of his character that we never would have known in the same way if evil hadn't entered the world.

For example, if we had not fallen into sin, if we had never failed to meet God's moral standards, how would we know and appreciate his unconditional love? How would we experience his mercy, grace, and forgiveness? We wouldn't. But God is so good that he is able to take our moral failures and use them to reveal further aspects of his greatness. That's amazing!

You might wonder how we will be free in heaven without the possibility of reintroducing evil and suffering. This side of heaven is our testing ground, our opportunity to freely place our faith in Jesus Christ. In eternity, having been washed clean by his blood, we will experience a New Eden, free from the possibility of moral failure.

But won't that make us like robots in heaven? Not at all. As a result of our trusting in Jesus, our nature in heaven will be glorified to the point that we will be impeccable. We will be fully like God in that sense: free, and yet *unable* to sin. We will have the agency to fully exercise our freedom, operating within the bounds of our renewed nature, yet without the possibility of sin. That's the gift every believer obtains by willingly trusting Christ.

Although the Bible tells us *how* evil and suffering entered the world, it doesn't go into detail about *why* God permitted these scourges to take root. Which isn't to say that God doesn't have a good reason for permitting it. It just means that we, as finite creatures, aren't privy to it. Moreover, just because God hasn't dealt with evil according to our timetable, it doesn't mean he *won't* deal with it in his own time. He will. The Cross is God's statement to the world that he has provided a way through his Son, Jesus, to ultimately deal with evil, suffering, and pain. By dying on the cross, Christ paved a way for every believer to begin their journey toward the New Eden, a celestial paradise that will be truly and forever free of all evil and suffering.

15

WHY DO CHRISTIANS MAKE SO MANY EXCUSES FOR GOD?

In our modern Western society, Christians often try to make excuses for God. They want to make Christianity acceptable in the eyes of their friends and peers. They want the world system to embrace Christianity. But true Christianity has always been a thorn in the side of humanistic world systems. It has always been counter-world culture.

GLENN DAVIS

Many people have understandably been confused by the story found in Genesis 22, where God tells Abraham to sacrifice his son Isaac. To be honest, if someone were to confide in me, "Pastor Bobby, I heard from God, and he wants me to present my son to him as a burnt offering," I'd call the police and think, *This one flew over the cuckoo's nest.*

So how do we explain such a request without making it seem as if God condones child sacrifice? It's certainly not enough to say something like, "Well, God works in mysterious ways," or "You just gotta have faith," or "Whatever God commands becomes good by the very fact of his commanding it." It's answers like these that can sound like we're making excuses for God, and I'm afraid such superficial answers would come off to the skeptic as a bit naive. But what if we were to explain that one purpose of God's command to Abraham was to *challenge* the religious practice of child sacrifice?

From my perspective, a better answer would go something like this:

I can understand why you are put off by the story of Abraham and Isaac. That was my initial reaction when I read Genesis 22 as well. It's hard to imagine a good God asking a father to kill his child, so you're right to ask the question. But did you know that at least one salient purpose of that event was to turn the common practice of child sacrifice on its head? As an accommodating God, the Lord meets people on their own turf—that is, he meets them where they are in order to bring them to where he is.

Remember that Abraham grew up in the Chaldean city of Ur, in Southern Mesopotamia. In that region of the ancient world, child sacrifice was how people demonstrated allegiance to their gods. Responding to the command to offer up Isaac gave Abraham an opportunity to demonstrate his total commitment to God.

But, as you know if you've read the story, at just the point when Abraham is about to slay his son, the angel of the Lord stops him. It's as if God is saying, "Stop, Abraham. I'm not like other gods." As the father of God's chosen people, Abraham had to know that child sacrifice was not acceptable to God.

There's no guarantee this answer will satisfy someone, but at least it provides a context for the command—that God, who never planned to accept Isaac as a sacrifice, was bringing that pagan religious practice to an end for Abraham.

Skeptics love to latch on to stories like the one of Abraham and Isaac and use them as leverage to shake the confidence of ill-equipped Christians. There has hardly been anyone more obnoxious in his attacks than the famed evolutionary biologist Richard

Dawkins. An oft-quoted passage from his book *The God Delusion* showcases his blistering criticism:

> The God of the Old Testament is arguably the most unpleasant character in all fiction: jealous and proud of it; a petty, unjust, unforgiving control-freak; a vindictive, bloodthirsty ethnic cleanser; a misogynistic, homophobic, racist, infanticidal, genocidal, filicidal, pestilential, megalomaniacal, sadomasochistic, capriciously malevolent bully.[1]

Dawkins's portrait of God saddens me. I'm pretty sure I can speak for my fellow Christians when I say, "If that's God, I'm not interested either." The truth, however, is that thoughtful Christians would not only beg to differ with Dawkins but would also be able to provide alternative ways to understand the disturbing passages that sparked his incendiary remarks.

But where does Dawkins derive his definition of *unjust* or *just*? Words such as *just, unjust, right,* and *wrong* all imply a *standard of measure.* But what's the standard within atheism? Where does Dawkins find his moral authority? Or, to pose the question differently, who is he to say that it's right or wrong to be jealous, proud, petty, unforgiving, and so on? Through the eyes of an atheist—that is, in a world without God—are we not all just beasts fending for ourselves? Isn't it all just survival of the fittest?

Each of Dawkins's challenges has its answer. And the answers make a lot of sense unpacked in their proper context. But if we want to provide answers that don't merely sound like excuses, we must take the time to properly understand the context of the ancient Near Eastern world in which the Bible was written.

Today, given the free-for-all on social media, skeptics are more than happy to take the Scriptures out of context and use condescending rhetoric to make believers feel silly for believing in God. But if we look past the rhetoric and properly unpack Scripture, in its original context, we can give credible answers instead of cop-out excuses. But let me offer two possible reasons why some Christians seem to make excuses for God:

1. *Christians make excuses for God because they aren't trained to give proper answers.* Unfortunately, many churches are led by pastors who downplay the need for apologetics and fail to equip their congregations to think astutely about the challenging questions facing the church today. Consequently, sincere believers on the front lines are doing the best they can, but too often they are ill-equipped to engage in the battle of ideas aimed at the church. I've often said that when people say apologetics are not important, they are simply revealing how little evangelism they are doing. Get out among unbelievers, and it won't take long before you are confronted with questions.

   Here's the agonizing truth: When pastors fail to equip their churches with apologetics, Christians are often left making excuses for God. They don't know what to say because they haven't been taught. Pastors can't just stick their heads in the sand. They are called to shepherd their flocks, and that requires teaching their congregations how to think, discern, and develop a worldview so they can be ready to provide answers to tough questions. It's our job as pastors to give people confidence to boldly engage the world in which we live.

   Sadly, many pastors have a distorted view of apologetics.

They fail to see that the New Testament is loaded with examples of people tirelessly contending for the faith. Can you imagine a drill sergeant sending his infantry off to war without first sending the would-be soldiers through boot camp? Or handing weapons over to his unit but never teaching them how to shoot? That wouldn't serve them well once they arrived on the front lines. And yet, that's what many of our pastors are doing with their congregations today. They tell them, "Believe the Bible," but fail to equip them to explain why God's Word is believable. Meanwhile, the church is being bombarded by a world of ideas, as we send our members to the front lines utterly ill-equipped to navigate the challenging rhetoric that is continuously being lobbed at them.

2. *Some professing Christians make excuses for God, not because they believe in him but because they fear his punishment if it turns out he exists.* Such people make excuses for God because they're afraid to admit they're lost. As I was reading online one day, I noticed a post from a skeptical blogger that captured this sentiment:

> I think for quite a few it traces back to their fear of hell far outweighing any sense of love for the biblical god. When pressed on the morality of the biblical god's actions, they will retreat into "He operates on a different morality that we can't understand," or "He's god, he can do anything he wants." . . .
>
> Better to just shut up about the character of the Christian god and play along, hope he doesn't

notice your internal doubts and you will slide into heaven. . . .

They think people like us who loudly object to Christianity are staking out a position that while possibly intellectually sound, might get them a one way ticket to hell.[2]

Such people are insincere; they don't believe, but to cover themselves for the possibility that they are wrong, they continue to make excuses for God. Whatever the case may be, God doesn't need us to try to justify his actions. If we are genuine followers of Christ, we should want to understand how to address the most challenging questions of our time. Not because we want to beat people up with the Bible, but because these people matter to God. We should care about their questions (even if they are insincere) in the hope that God will use us to help them see the truthfulness of our beliefs. God never asked us to cover for him, but he does expect us to be equipped and prepared to defend the truthfulness of our faith.[3]

16

HOW CAN A GOOD GOD ALLOW US TO SUFFER?

God whispers to us in our pleasures, speaks in our conscience, but shouts in our pain: it is His megaphone to rouse a deaf world.

C. S. LEWIS

When I was in high school, the students were required to visit a local nursing home as a service project to spend time with the elderly. At first, I was hesitant, but then I met an elderly fellow named Nathan, who was clearly at the end of his rope, and we hit it off. I'd drop in periodically to play cards and smoke cigarettes with him. And boy, did Nathan love his cigarettes. As soon as he finished one, he would look at me plaintively and say in his weak and haunted-house-sounding voice, "Smooooke." I would cave almost immediately and fire up another one for him, even though I felt guilty for helping him exceed his daily limit.

After I became a Christian and felt the call to preach, memories of my times with Nathan stuck with me—so much so that, during Bible college, I asked the staff at a local convalescent home if

I could come by each week to connect with the elderly and share a brief message of hope. They graciously agreed. This became a great place for me to develop as a young preacher. I would show up, connect with the elderly residents, and then bust out my old boom box to play a few hymns before closing with a brief lesson from the Bible.

There were some special moments I joyfully remember. The first had to do with an elderly woman who was mean as a hornet. (When I looked up the word *curmudgeon* in the dictionary, her picture was there alongside the definition.) She would complain, slap the old men around, and get feisty. Everyone knew to steer clear when she got going. I was tempted to think, *God, I know you parted the Red Sea and all, but I'm not sure even you can save this one.*

One day, as I was preaching away, I saw her walking toward me with the nastiest of looks.

Alarmed, I said to myself, *I think I'm about to receive an uppercut.*

But that's not what happened. Not even close. Unexpectedly, in front of everyone, this hard-bitten woman looked at me and shouted out as serious as can be, "I WANNA GET SAVED!"

Stunned, and hardly knowing what to say in response, I looked around the room and blurted out, "Folks, she wants to get saved." And just like that, I stopped my message and led her to Christ. As you can imagine, that was a special moment for me as a young preacher.

There's one other person I'd like to tell you about from this nursing home. I don't recall his name, but I remember the impact this elderly fellow had on my life. He was a model of suffering well.

Typically when we suffer, our first thought is to look for a means of escape: "How can I get out of this?" What I learned from this elderly gentleman is that we *should* be asking instead, "*What* can I get out of this?" I'm talking about character, patience, perspective, and faithful endurance—the good stuff we often learn best through suffering.

Some people handle suffering better and more graciously than others. This man sat beautifully. Confined to a wheelchair, he couldn't speak, he couldn't walk, he couldn't even eat on his own. Yet his life made a tremendous difference. As he sat with his head slumped over his chest, he still found a way, whenever he saw me, to send me a smile. Not only that, but he would struggle mightily to lift his arm to show me the picture he carried in the palm of his hand. It was a picture of Jesus. That's right.

This man, who was seemingly at the end of his earthly lifeline, when everything else was stripped away, still found a way to give us Jesus. To many people, it would seem that this gentleman had nothing left to offer, but there he was, day after day, offering what mattered most: Jesus. Talk about a model of suffering well. This man taught me something very powerful about the goodness of God. To this day, his memory serves as a continuous reminder that God is good, no matter how much suffering or evil we encounter in the world.

In a world where so many people question God's goodness when they suffer, this man carried a picture of Jesus—the source of his comfort—in the palm of his hand. It was Jesus who gave him the strength to persevere. And it was Jesus, the suffering servant, who gave him the proper perspective, enabling him to joyfully handle his own suffering. In a world where so many people are disillusioned about God because of pain and suffering, this old saint chose to see Jesus as the source of his comfort through trying times.

He didn't get bitter. He didn't doubt. He didn't deny God's goodness. Nor did he blame God for his troubles. Instead, he sat peacefully, bound to his wheelchair, with his chin slumped over his chest, reflecting Jesus to everyone he met. Yes, that gentle old soul was a great reminder that, even when life has seemingly taken everything away from us, we can remain joyful . . . because we still have Jesus, who promised to always be with us.[1] Regardless of how diminished his life appeared, this man of many days concluded that God is still good.

Circumstances change for all of us, but God's character remains true. Our *perspective* makes all the difference.

THE ONE-WAY-TO-SALVATION ISSUES

17

HOW CAN JESUS BE THE ONLY WAY TO HEAVEN WHEN SO MANY HAVE NEVER HEARD OF HIM?

Our awareness of "religious others" has never been more acute than it is today, forcing the church to deal with new and troubling questions that pose formidable challenges to traditional Christian beliefs and practices.

HAROLD NETLAND

In 2011, I visited India for the first time. As we drove through various villages and towns in northern India, I couldn't get one haunting question off my mind: *Have all the people who ever lived in this region gone to hell simply because they never heard about Jesus?* This thought tore me apart the whole time I was there, and I distinctly remember looking out the window of the airplane as I flew home, viscerally unsettled by doubt as I kept mulling over that question.

At some point during the flight, God gently probed me with the thought, *Bobby, if you care this much about these people and worry about their ultimate destiny, how much more do you think I care?* Somehow that simple impression alleviated some of my inner agony, but I was still looking for answers. How could I find peace about the destiny of all those people without forfeiting the exclusive claim of Christ, who said, "I am the way and the truth and the life. No one comes to the Father except through me"?[1] I knew I had to come to terms with this dilemma if I were ever to find my way out of the maze of doubt.

Understandably, the exclusive claims of Christ often serve as a great excuse for skeptics looking for a reason to reject Christianity. And yet it's not as if exclusive claims are unique to Christianity. As I thought about it, I realized that every belief system is exclusive in its own way. Atheists say there is no God, and if you believe in God, or many gods, you're wrong. Isn't that exclusive? Relativists maintain that truth is relative to the individual, and if you claim that truth is absolute, you're wrong. Isn't that exclusive? Agnostics say we can't know whether God exists, so if you say he either does or he doesn't, you're wrong. Isn't that exclusive?

Even the polytheists are exclusive. They believe in many gods, but if you say God doesn't exist or claim there is only one God, they will accuse you of being wrong. Isn't that also exclusive? At last, I could see that the issue isn't about *exclusivity*; it's about *truth*. Which one of these many competing beliefs is true? As a Christian apologist and formerly tormented doubter regarding this question, I will share with you how I came to a place of rest, both mentally and emotionally, on the issue of exclusivity.

People have put forth various views to explain the fate of those who have never heard about Jesus. *Universalists* believe that everyone will ultimately end up in heaven. *Inclusivists* teach that Christianity is the only true religion but concede that salvation can be extended to sincere Muslims, Buddhists, and Hindus, all of whom might enjoy the presence of God in heaven one day. In addition to these views, there are two versions of *exclusivism*, hard and soft.

Hard exclusivists teach that people are lost forever apart from hearing and accepting the gospel story about the death and resurrection of Jesus. This was the view that ruffled my feathers in India. *Soft exclusivism*, which is the view I believe makes the best sense of the biblical data, teaches that one's salvation is always and only on account of Christ and his atoning work; therefore, people who have never *heard* the gospel message but who respond positively to God's general revelation in creation (Romans 1) and conscience (Romans 2) may possibly be saved apart from specific knowledge of Christ—even though they are explicitly saved on the basis of Christ's atoning death. That is my hope.

Unlike the inclusivists, who are willing to grant a pass to people of other faith traditions, provided they hold to the aspects of truth in their own belief systems that cohere with Christianity, soft exclusivists do not accept that people who have *committed* themselves to another belief system—such as Islam, Buddhism, or Hinduism—can be saved on account of what those beliefs promise.

Suppose someone has never heard the gospel but cries out to God, saying, "I'm not sure who you are, but by faith I believe you created the universe, and I believe you are a good God and that I have failed to live up to your moral expectations for me. Will you forgive me?" What does this person's prayer entail? Recognition that God is the Creator and that he is good. Acknowledgment that the person has sinned, along with a prayerful act of faith that asks for pardon. If someone has never heard the gospel, read the Bible, or had a dream or vision or some type of mystical encounter with God, would this prayer suffice? I believe that God could choose to save that person on account of their faith, in light of what Christ accomplished through his atonement, even though the person remains in the dark regarding that historic event.

Under the Old Covenant, this is exactly how some people outside the covenant community were made right with God. By faith, they responded to general revelation—that is, the revelation of God for all humanity, as detected through both conscience and creation. Are we to imagine that, at the very moment Christ said *tetelestai* ("It is finished"), those geographically out of reach for hundreds of years to come could no longer be made right with God due to their lack of proximity to the Holy Land?

Think about it. Would the person in India (or elsewhere) who responded to general revelation and was able to get right with God the moment before Christ drew his final breath be in a different position one moment *after* Christ's final breath—perpetually destined to hell only because he or she was ignorant of what had taken place on Good Friday?

In the same way that God held people accountable for the knowledge they had under the Old Covenant, is it not fair to hope that he would operate similarly under the New Covenant? Otherwise, millions of people will spend an eternity apart from Christ on account of a message they never heard. Does that seem just?

I don't believe the gospel is compromised in the least if someone genuinely responds by faith to general revelation, as disclosed in creation (Psalm 19; Romans 1:20) and conscience (Romans 2:14–15). If this condition still stands, people in this position could be saved in a manner similar to those under the Old Covenant who weren't familiar with what Christ would accomplish on the cross.

There is one final objection I must set aside before wrapping up this chapter. Some may say, "If people can be saved apart from hearing the gospel, why bother sharing Christ with those who have never heard?" Because becoming a Christian includes so much more than simply bypassing hell. The gospel is a way of life, and the more revelation we have, the more in sync we can live with the New Covenant way. Not only that, but if a person were truly to respond by faith to general revelation, it is my belief that this same person would also affirm the gospel message if given the chance to hear it. In other words, the gospel would resonate as the truth this person had been searching for. By reaching unreached people, we give them a far greater opportunity to receive all that God has in store for them through his revealed word.

If you have wrestled with this question as I have, my hope is that this brief consideration of soft exclusivism will help you discover a scripturally uncompromising way forward that can reconcile the dilemma of how one might possibly be saved through Christ without having heard the content of the gospel.

18

HOW CAN A LOVING GOD SEND PEOPLE TO HELL?

The only place outside Heaven where you can be perfectly safe from all the dangers and perturbations of love is Hell.

C. S. LEWIS

When I moved to Arkansas, it was impossible for me to miss how ingrained Christianity was in the culture there. One clue was the number of massive, roadside billboards inquiring, "Where are you going? Heaven or hell?" or the dilapidated marquee signs, many of which looked as if they hadn't been repaired since the middle of the last century, touting cheesy truisms like, "Seven days without prayer makes one weak."

Then there was the controversy over which version of the Bible one should use, and some people became seriously agitated if you read any version other than the King James. I encountered this firsthand while attending a country church in rural Arkansas. During my visit, I met an elderly gentleman who boasted about a recent bonfire his church had hosted. This was not a hot dogs and s'mores kind of event. No, this was a *Bible* bonfire. Talk about redefining BYOB.

Apparently, congregants were told to bring their non-KJV Bibles and commit them to the flames, which they did. I can only imagine how proud God must have been to see that. When I heard this, I couldn't stay silent. Looking straight into the old man's face, I affected a faux Southern accent and said, "Well, y'all done burned the version of the Bible God used to change my life." You could've heard a pin drop as he looked at me with an awkward smile. That's what you call a "you gotta be kidding me!" moment. I'm still shocked.

I also remember a popular form of church outreach at the time, called Hell House. This was a Christian alternative to Halloween. The idea behind these events was for Christians to bring their nonbelieving friends to a haunted house–type setup with the goal of—wait for it—scaring the hell out of them. And of course, at least secondarily, for people to place their faith in Christ. As curiosity got the best of me, I took Heather to experience a live Hell House. As we entered, it was like being cast into Dante's inferno.

We passed several eerie scenes along the way, including a walk down a dark hallway strewn with red lights and periodic demons to surprise us. We encountered various people writhing in the torture chamber of hell, each purportedly guilty of some awful sin. Then there were the radioactive spiders that crept through the hallways, along with yellow caution tape, people mourning around caskets, creepy music, Satan dressed up like the lead singer from Kiss, and even some dude firing up a chainsaw. At last, there was light at the end of the tunnel. Angels arrayed in long white robes marked the way to the sanctuary, where visitors soon encountered Jesus and there learned how to escape the nightmare of hell they had supposedly just experienced. If you so desired, you could acquire your own Hell House kit to bring a show to a church near you.

No matter how you cut it, the reality of hell is not an easy doctrine to digest. In fact, no other doctrine in all of Scripture has caused me more turmoil. I suppose that's the way it should be. This was acutely true for me as a young believer, when I was taught that the language Jesus used to describe hell was to be taken literally. The thought of people caught up forever in flames was unbearable for a person who doesn't do well on a hot, humid day in the South. Even though I no longer interpret *fire*, *outer darkness*, and *weeping and gnashing of teeth* as literal—viewing them instead as metaphorical descriptions of the horrifying reality of being eternally separated from God—it still doesn't eliminate the discomfort I feel when I contemplate the fate of the unsaved.

No wonder so many people are curious as to how a loving God could consign people to such an eternal condition. Even though my answer won't erase the gruesome reality of everlasting damnation, I hope it can clarify some of the confusion. Let's begin with the love part of the equation, as it relates to God's justice. In the West, we have an incomplete view of love. For some reason, it's hard for many Westerners to envision a God of unconditional love without stripping him of his ultimate justice. But true love is just.

And yet, there are those who would be quick to reply, "But the punishment doesn't fit the crime. How can a just God punish people forever for sins they committed in a temporal life?" That's a reasonable question. Some would say it's because our mortal sins were committed against an eternal God, but I don't find that argument very compelling. God can't help but be eternal, any more than we, in our earthly state, can help but be temporal. It seems too much of a stretch to suggest that, based on God's eternal nature, temporal beings who fail to believe the gospel will be eternally punished.

An answer that makes better sense to me is one I've heard William Lane Craig give on several occasions. He says that the reason hell goes on forever is that sinning goes on forever. He might be on to something here. It's not as if people will suddenly become sinless upon arriving in hell. In fact, they're likely to sin even more there. And unlike on earth, God's general grace—the grace he extends to believers and nonbelievers alike—won't be at work in hell. Hell is where humanity's fallen nature will come to full bloom. And it won't be pretty. The lost will discover what human depravity is really all about. In this literally godforsaken setting, humanity's addiction to sin will be unfettered. But the supposed pleasures of sin will disappear. In his love, God has gone to great lengths to spare us the reality of hell—through Christ's sacrificial death on the cross. No one *must* go there . . . but, sadly, many will.

Another aspect of the question that must be addressed has to do with the idea that God *sends* people to hell. Hell is not a place that God sends people against their will. Rather, hell is peopled by those who have consciously rejected God's free and universal offer of salvation. The Scriptures pointedly state that everyone will be without excuse.[1] In other words, God's justice will be vindicated. We can take comfort in knowing that God is "not willing that any should perish."[2] The bigger problem is that some people aren't willing to embrace God's offer of salvation through Christ.

Far from consigning people to hell, God sent his only begotten Son to purchase salvation for us so that we could bypass hell altogether. Tragically, that's not good enough for some people. As C. S. Lewis aptly put it, "Never fear. There are only two kinds of people in the end: those who say to God, 'Thy will be done,' and those to whom God says, in the end, '*Thy* will be done.' All that are in Hell, choose it."[3] The devastating truth is not that God doesn't want everyone to be saved, but rather that some people just don't want God—at least not the God of the Bible. It isn't that God doesn't love all people; it's just that some people don't love God. Nor is it that God doesn't want all people in heaven; it's just that some people don't want to be in heaven with God.

Hell is a hard topic to think about, but it's really not all that hard to imagine. If I were to ask, "Do you think anyone has ever lived who deserves hell?" most people could think of at least one. I'm sure I'd hear names like Hitler and Stalin, as well as those of serial killers, pedophiles, and others of similar ilk. If I were to push further and inquire, "Why them?" I'd begin hearing about their moral atrocities. But you see what's happening, right? We can envision hell for people who fit the criteria we deem appropriate. The problem is that we're using the wrong standard for judging. We are using *our own* standard, whereas the standard by which *everyone* will be judged is God's righteous and holy yardstick. If we're being honest, the hardest reality to swallow about hell isn't the thought of someone like Hitler going there; it's people like *us*.

I suppose there's no easy answer when it comes to hell, nor should there be. But we'd be wise to remember that God is perfectly just; he's not willing that any should perish, and he has gone to great lengths to save us, as demonstrated by his sending Jesus to die on a cross for us. He has been more than patient with us, but he has assured us that, in the final analysis, no one will be without excuse for a negative response to Jesus. Though that's certainly not the only or primary reason for trusting Christ, it should give us some motivation.

19

DOES THE RISE OF THE NONES MEAN THE INSTITUTIONAL CHURCH IS OBSOLETE?

Christians now outnumber religious "nones" by a ratio of a little more than two-to-one. In 2007, when the Center began asking its current question about religious identity, Christians outnumbered "nones" by almost five-to-one (78 percent vs. 16 percent).

2021 PEW RESEARCH CENTER STUDY

The first time I heard the phrase "the nones are on the rise," I thought to myself, *That's weird: The nuns are on the rise?* Of course, I quickly learned that it wasn't a reference to Catholic nuns; rather, "nones" is a term coined to describe those with "no religious affiliation." People who check "none" when asked about their religious affiliation now comprise a rapidly growing demographic in the United States, with nearly three out of ten adults identifying as such. In fact, according to a Pew Research poll released in 2021, the number of nones has quadrupled since the study's genesis in 2007. At that time, a mere 7 percent of Americans identified as nones, with numbers soaring to 29 percent by 2021.[1] Though the nones category includes atheists and agnostics, those categorized as "unchurched" are also lumped in.

The unchurched may still believe in God and hold to various spiritual beliefs, but they reject organized religion.

What's with All the Nones?

Even more alarming than the overall percentages, this growing trend includes large numbers of nones who are now young adults but grew up in the church, only to opt out at some point after leaving home. It may be due to a lack of discipleship in both the home and the church, but when the time came to leave the nest, many of these kids weren't ready to encounter a world that was more than ready to help them begin their journey away from the church. If we are going to retain our young people in the church, we must disciple them toward a fully orbed Christian worldview that prepares them for life beyond the shelter provided by Mom and Dad. They need something more than entertainment at church. Lord knows, they're getting plenty of that. They need to be equipped to live in the world without selling out. Filling this deficit will require intentional action, not only in the church but also in the home, along with strategic partnerships between churches and families to better ensure that these kids will be equipped to withstand the threats awaiting them in college and the workplace.

Besides a lack of discipleship, there are other contributing factors leading to the rise of the nones, including a breakdown of the American family; the individualistic spirit of American society; a false sense of security brought about by increased wealth; progressive education that challenges established Christian beliefs; traumatic church experiences for some; the mental health crisis; and of course, the rapid secularization of our nation.

As political science professor Ryan Burge writes,

The reality is simply this: Americans used to be Christians simply by default. Secularization merely gave permission for a lot of people to express who they truly are—religiously unaffiliated. . . .

While nearly 1 in 4 Americans no longer [affiliate] with religion, just 1 in 10 Americans [do] not believe God exists. The issue is not that interest in spiritual matters has declined; it's that people do not want to label themselves.[2]

The gap between *unaffiliated* and *atheist* suggests that a large part of the growth of the nones is driven by people disillusioned with the church. Why is that? Apart from the issues listed above, the mass exodus from the church is deeply rooted in a growing disdain for organized religion. This leaves us with the question we now must answer: Isn't the rise of the nones evidence that the institutional church is obsolete?

For starters, *relevance* and *popularity* are not the same thing. Though a drastic drop in church attendance warrants consideration, the numerical shift alone tells us nothing about the relevance of Christianity. It simply indicates people's current level of interest. We don't always understand the importance of faith, even as we reduce its role in our lives.

Let me offer an example that might help to clarify the point.

If reading became less popular and the number of people who know how to read plummeted from 95 percent to 75 percent, it wouldn't make literacy any less important. It would simply mean that many people were lacking a vital life skill. In the same way, when we see that less than half of US adults pray daily, it's not because prayer doesn't matter as much as it used to; it just means that people are now neglecting an important spiritual habit.

So what can be done about the rise of the nones?

1. *The exodus from the church and the rise of the nones can help the church explore why it is struggling to retain its flock.* Churches with a keen eye can adjust their approach to more proactively address the concerns that are causing people to bail out and offer them reasons to stay—and grow—through proper Christian discipleship.

2. *The church can reevaluate what it means to be the church.* Far too many churches have become overly institutionalized. The church is meant to be an organism, not an organization. Certainly, the organism must be organized, but all too often the church looks, runs, and feels more like a business than a connected body of believers tethered around a Great Commission vision. I recall a conversation I had with a man who had been burned by the bureaucracy in his church. The church was a well-oiled machine, but to him it felt lifeless, all business, and so planned out that there was no room left for God to work off-script. Having left for another local congregation, he said of his previous church, "The Holy Spirit could've departed six months ago, and they wouldn't know it."

The church is not a perfect place. It's messy. It has its problems. But running away is not the solution. Instead, we must dig in and help to revive it. I'm not talking about buildings and programs. I'm referring to *a body of believers* joined together in common purpose. It is a *connected* body that is meant to be together and whose togetherness often happens in a building. After all, we have to be together *somewhere*, right? The author of Hebrews put it bluntly: "Let us not neglect our meeting together, as some people do, but encourage one another, especially now that the day of [Christ's] return is drawing near."[3] This is no time to abandon ship; instead, it's time to repair the ship and make it see-worthy. No, that's not a typo. We need to give disillusioned people a fresh look at the church—something worth seeing and becoming a part of.

As tempting as it might be to panic, there is a positive way to view the shrinking numbers in the church. Perhaps God is separating the wheat from the chaff. It costs people something to be part of the church—their reputation. It's no longer considered cool to be a Christian. But Jesus' invitation for us to take up our cross still stands.[4] During COVID, I found myself feeling pretty discouraged at how quickly the church was thinning out. But I found great encouragement when I let Jesus' words to Peter sink in: "I will build my church, and the gates of hell shall not prevail against it."[5] That verse hit me like a ton of bricks.

When all is said and done, nothing will cause the *true* church—those that Christ calls his own—to shrink.[6] Not atheism. Not COVID-19. Not secularism. And not the nones. Whatever Satan lobs our way, be it hell itself, it won't stop Jesus from building his true church, whatever the seeming status of the organized, visible church at any point. So be encouraged, Christian. All of this winnowing may be preparing the way for the world to get a real look at God through the window of his pure and unadulterated bride, the church.

The next time you feel discouraged about the shrinking church, remember that Jesus is still in the redemption business, and his promise to grow his church is still in effect. Though the numbers may be declining right now in America, the Great Commission is still bearing fruit all over the world. Wherever we are, we must continue to avail ourselves to bring in the harvest as God allows.[7] We can be assured that Christ will continue to build his church.

20

CAN'T I BE SPIRITUAL WITHOUT BEING A CHRISTIAN?

[When online dating first became popular], "spiritual-but-not-religious" became a nice category that said, "I'm not some kind of cold-hearted atheist, but I'm not some kind of moralizing, prudish person, either. I'm nice, friendly, and spiritual—but not religious."

MATTHEW HEDSTROM

"Spiritual but not religious" (SBNR) has become a catchphrase among people who don't want to identify with any particular religion. It sounds deep, but what does it mean? It's hard to capture a common spirit among the SBNRs, partly because they are anti-dogma, which means that the sky is the limit when it comes to defining their terms. For some, *spiritual* may mean that they recognize the limits of the material universe and therefore look to the immaterial, unseen realm to capture a sense of belonging. For others, it may amount to a simple acknowledgment that the material world is all that exists but that science fails to address some of the deeper existential questions of life, related to meaning, value, and purpose.

That is why certain atheists can describe themselves as spiritual while still rejecting the supernatural. For others, being spiritual is a matter of "being" versus "doing." It's less about *place*—such as taking a trip to India or visiting Sedona—and more about practicing *presence*, living in the here and now.

Then there are those spirituals who are disillusioned with religion and have sought to shed all things creedal, at the same time retaining a mystical connection to the divine. For some spirituals, the definition may imply that they care about certain values, such as being open-minded, demonstrating world compassion, showing empathy toward others, or wearing a peace cross.

All that to say there is no one-size-fits-all version of spirituality. Those who identify as spiritual may use this designation because they are into exfoliating as they listen to spa music; attending to the surrealistic art of Vladimir Kush; practicing yoga; sitting in silence with spurts of humming; attending nature retreats with journal in hand; meditating in a lotus position; looking at horoscopes; fasting; detoxing and cleansing; or quietly walking the dog. What draws many to the "I'm spiritual" mantra is the flexibility the term offers without locking them into a particular brand of religion.

But be ready for this. When someone says, "I'm spiritual, but not religious," they are typically unified with others in their distaste for institutionalized religion, doctrine, and all forms of church hierarchy. Consider this explanation from an article published in *The Atlantic*:

> Americans are leaving organized religion in droves:
> they disagree with their churches on political issues;
> they feel restricted by dogma; they're deserting formal
> organizations of all kinds. Instead of atheism, however,

they're moving toward an identity captured by the term "spirituality." Approximately sixty-four million Americans—one in five—identify as "spiritual but not religious," or SBNR.[1]

Many of those who fall into the SBNR category believe they don't need to be a Christian in order to be spiritual. But how should we think about this? Is it possible to be spiritual without adhering to a formal religion or belief system? Let's navigate this question together.

First of all, if you're ever asked the question, "Can I be spiritual without being a Christian?" I suggest you start by requesting clarification: "What do you mean by 'spiritual'?" As we've seen, there is a wide array of spiritualities out there, so it's helpful to know the person's definition.

What people typically mean is that there is more to the world than meets the eye. There is an unseen realm that these individuals are trying to tap into. Some envision themselves as spiritual beings trapped in a physical experience, which we call material reality. Typically, when someone says they are spiritual but not religious, they subscribe to an amalgamation of spiritual beliefs—which, upon closer inspection, may even contradict each other. This is the epitome of syncretism. It's more about *feeling* right than *being* right. It's less about *knowing* and more about *experiencing*. It's more circular than linear, more organic than orderly, and more subjective than objective.

We must learn to discern between pseudo-spirituality and authentic spirituality, as the Bible does. The apostle Paul, in one of his letters to the church in Corinth, sets the record straight about what it means to be truly spiritual:

This is what we speak, not in words taught us by human wisdom but in words taught by the Spirit, explaining spiritual realities with Spirit-taught words. The person without the Spirit does not accept the things that come from the Spirit of God but considers them foolishness, and cannot understand them because they are discerned only through the Spirit.[2]

What, exactly, is foolish to the natural person? The gospel of Jesus Christ. As Paul exclaims, "The message of the cross is foolishness to those who are perishing, but to us who are being saved it is the power of God." And who are those "who are being saved"? It is those who have embraced the gospel of Jesus Christ, who have been born of the Spirit and thus are truly spiritual.

In order to be truly *spiritual*, a person needs a spiritual awakening, a new birth experience, a born-again encounter with God. That doesn't mean we're without defect after our salvation experience. We all have our share of bumps and bruises. But it does mean we have been made right with God. In this temporal realm, we will always be works in progress, because the sanctifying Holy Spirit is continually at work in us to bring about our ultimate glorification through Jesus.

In our culture, *spirituality* is a soupy word. It represents a mishmash of ideas from which people can customize their own brand. People can burn incense; play with beads; attempt to levitate; read tarot cards; fondle crystals; obsess over the Zodiac; boil mushrooms; sip teas; munch on edibles; be vegan; grow their own gardens; drive a Subaru; stare at trees; care for their pets; drink from paper straws; celebrate national hemp day; eliminate toxins; avoid bad vibes; talk to their lightworkers, shamans, or personal gurus; or listen to Deepak Chopra, Oprah Winfrey, Eckhart Tolle, and the Dalai Lama. People can do all these things (and more) as much as they want, but make no mistake—apart from the work of the Holy Spirit, any claim to spirituality is a thin veneer of the bona fide spirituality that comes through the foolish gospel of Jesus Christ.

THE SCIENCE PROBLEM

21

ISN'T SCIENCE ABOUT FACTS AND RELIGION ABOUT FAITH?

The success of the West, including the rise of science, rested entirely on religious foundations, and the people who brought it about were devout Christians.

RODNEY STARK

There's a sharp young man in my church (I'll call him Jake) who is always ready for a good philosophical debate. It's not uncommon for him to hit me up with a challenging question after a Sunday message. At times he struggles to reconcile his faith in Jesus with his understanding of science. That's why he was so eager to ask me one morning, "Isn't science about facts and religion about faith?" For Jake, as for a lot of people, science just makes sense. At times he finds it hard to relate to the Bible, especially to its miraculous components. During our conversation, he expressed a desire for his faith to mesh with his scientific knowledge, even as he expressed concern that the two seemed to be in conflict.

What do you say to someone like that?

For starters, it's important to let people know that they're not alone. Lots of believers have asked the same questions. And, fortunately, there are plenty of thoughtful, scientifically minded Christians to whom we can turn for direction. That said, Christians tend to be all over the map on how to reconcile faith and science.

Ken Boa and Robert Bowman Jr., in their helpful book *Faith Has Its Reasons*, consider four primary ways in which apologists have approached this question.[1] Let's call them four schools of thought. The following apologetic approaches are not intended to fully explain the various theories, but simply to depict how each school of thought addresses the faith and science question.

Reformed Apologists

According to Boa and Bowman, some Christians contend that faith and science are in conflict and that Christians should exercise extreme caution when trying to take their cues from the Bible through scientific discovery. That's because we live in a world that utilizes a scientific method of discovery that largely excludes God from the process. As it relates to an apologetic approach, people in this camp are often called *reformed apologists*. They recognize an inherent danger in trying to muster up knowledge to strengthen their faith from a world that excludes God. Not surprisingly, advocates of this position often tend to be young-earth creationists.

Fideist Apologists

Fideist apologists argue that faith and science aren't in conflict, but neither do they cohere, because each field sets out to answer a different set of questions. Fideists are quick to point out that the Bible was constructed in a prescientific world, whereas science approaches its fieldwork with an entirely different mindset.

Believers who hold to this view can fall into both young- and old-earth categories, but many adhere to some version of theistic evolution.

Evidentialist Apologists

Other Christians leverage science as a tool to better understand their faith, while equally recognizing that science is in a continuous state of developmental flux. *Evidentialist apologists* recognize the need to remain open to fine-tuning their discoveries in the event that a new finding happens to modify or replace an old theory. They keep their eye on the evidence and hold their conclusions loosely. For evidentialists, periodic updates are not a compromise to their faith but rather a simple recognition that the scientific enterprise, as it relates to the field of knowledge, continues to develop. That's not to say that science drives their interpretation of the Bible, but only to acknowledge their openness to embracing scientific findings insofar as they can be reconciled with Scripture. Obviously, one can see why many evidentialist apologists also subscribe to some version of old-earth creation theory.

Classical Apologists

Finally, there are the *classical apologists*, who glean evidence from scientific findings to support their faith, but do so with caution. They are quick to keep the Bible front and center, so that if a scientific viewpoint changes, they haven't put all of their eggs into one scientific basket. Classical apologists believe that God gave the world two books: the supernatural book called the Bible and the natural book called creation. The former is infallible, but theories about the latter are sometimes fallible; hence their cautionary approach to leveraging the best that science has to offer while simultaneously acknowledging that discoverers can be wrong about their hypotheses. Typically, classical apologists defend some version of old-earth creationism, but they're especially interested in discussing apologetic arguments from nature. For example, the cosmological and teleological arguments can often serve to help skeptics see the credibility of theism, while reinforcing the Christian's confidence that faith and science aren't at odds. As we can see, there are plenty of fruitful lanes one can intellectually drive down to better envision how science can inform our faith.

If God Exists, Miracles Are Possible

There are a lot of people like Jake in our churches today. They are sharp and believe in Jesus, but they often struggle to reconcile their belief in God with science. Some of this conflict relates to how they were taught—either in public-school classrooms by teachers who shunned belief in God, or in church by pastors who encouraged them to always mistrust science. Believers like Jake can benefit from much of what science has to offer, while realizing that science has its limits.

Sometimes Jake has a hard time relating to the miraculous. This is an area in which science won't assist him much. He'd be better served by studying arguments for God's existence and coming to terms with what those arguments imply. At bare minimum, these arguments showcase a powerful God who is well-equipped to intervene in the world he has created. If God exists, then miracles are possible. If he created the universe to begin with, he can tinker with it afterward. After all, it's his creation. Someone like Jake may also find help studying the historical case for the Resurrection. Although this endeavor is not a scientific study, the Resurrection is a well-documented historical event with more than enough material for Jake to ponder. This type of intellectual research could help Jake in his attempt to sand down the mental conflict he's experiencing between his faith in miracles and the world of science.

Presenting Live Options

As Christians, we need to give people like Jake options to consider. Mandating that a Christian can only be a young-earth creationist for fear of losing someone to science is neither wise nor helpful. If we are going to effectively lead people, I've found this will sometimes mean helping them find another way, even if it's not the way *we* would choose. I'd hate for Jake to fall into the hands of an overly zealous young-earth creationist whose only reply is, "Well, you obviously don't believe the Bible, and that's your real problem."

In no way am I trying to pick on young-earth creationists. I've met many who are kind, compassionate, and reasonably minded. And yet we acknowledge the predicament that a trite answer like the one above could present for someone like Jake. Let's face it. The world is filled with disillusioned faith-seekers who have left the church, believing there was no other option. Just think how some of these inquirers might have been helped along the way, had they been given a chance to consider other live options. That's called intellectual integrity. We owe it to people to be honest about alternative positions—especially those that square with Christianity.

What's most important is not how old or young Jake reckons the universe to be, but that he entrusts his life to Jesus. Our goal when someone like Jake addresses us is to help him keep his faith intact. Ancillary issues—like the age of the earth, the timing of Christ's return, or which Bible version one reads—should not be used as a litmus test of genuine faith. By introducing doubters to alternative ways in which Christian theologians and philosophers have thought about these topics, we can hope to allay their doubts and nudge them toward faith.

Dispelling the Myth

We can also help those wrestling with the question of whether faith and science are in conflict by pointing them to the great Christian scientists who have gone before us. Many of the best scientists of the past saw no conflict between faith and science. Consider religious believers such as Galileo, Copernicus, Faraday, Kepler, Boyle, and Newton, each of whom was devoted to scientific endeavors and belief in God. One might argue that this was because intellectual lights like them were products of their own epochs, and perhaps they would have believed differently had they lived today.

To begin with, that's an argument one could never prove. Not only that, but it isn't as if we're hard-pressed to identify solid scientists today who also believe in God. Many laureates in physics, chemistry, and medicine over the past century have identified as Christians. In fact, it has been estimated that 65.4 percent of Nobel Prize winners between 1901 and 2000 were Christians or had a Christian background.[2] That's an impressive statistic. And it certainly dispels the myth that good scientists don't believe in God.

Arguing that one cannot be both a genuine scientist and a genuine Christian is simply a canard that has been widely dismissed by historians of science today. That's not to say there aren't those who disagree. The world will likely always have militant atheists like Daniel Dennett, Richard Dawkins, Lawrence Krauss, and Peter Atkins. But these guys are vastly outnumbered by others in their field.[3] Intellectually honest scientists are more than willing to acknowledge the fruitful work of their Christian colleagues.

As I conclude this chapter, let me offer some encouragement to Jake and others who might be doubting the compatibility of faith and science. Christianity and science *both* deal in the realm of facts and faith. Faith is not simply a leap into the dark, a crossing of one's fingers, or wishful thinking. Faith is trust. And solid faith entrusts itself to solid facts. As Christians, we believe in the facts of Christ's resurrection, our own sin, and God's existence, and in light of these convictions, we place our faith in God, believing that the reasons provided in support of these facts are valid. So, too, with the scientists. They believe in the realities of energy and consciousness, acknowledge the existence of other minds and perspectives, and entrust themselves by faith to the reasons they give in support of these facts.

It doesn't have to be either/or. If the evidence is solid, our faith is on solid ground.

22

HASN'T ATHEISM BURIED GOD?

God is dead, God remains dead,
and we have killed him.

FRIEDRICH NIETZSCHE

In the mid-1990s, I worked with an older British man named Alan at a school furniture manufacturer in Conway, Arkansas. We both worked security and scouted out the premises to ensure that there was no suspicious activity. During our shifts inside the security booth, we delved into some lively conversations. Alan was an outspoken atheist who had no problem articulating his problems with religion. To him, the concept of God was nothing more than a human fabrication, an invention conjured up from the past. And he felt it was high time for me to update my beliefs and toss aside my faith in God.

As a fresh young convert, I was clearly overmatched by the age and experience gap, but that didn't faze me. Alan was miserable, and his face said it all. I reasoned, *If his worldview makes him that miserable, then I'm not interested.* He was a classic critic, with zero fear of God. I was shocked at how comfortable he was uttering blasphemous thoughts. He was perhaps the most convinced atheist I have ever encountered. At least he came off that way.

Although Alan surely thought I was fanciful and naive to believe in God, he liked me as a person, and for that I was thankful. And the feeling was mutual. Despite his miserable persona, my heart went out to him. I really liked the old curmudgeon. That's why it hurt a little bit more when I found out just a few months after leaving my job that cancer had run its course on him in a matter of weeks.

For Alan, Christianity just didn't make sense. Science was the be-all and end-all. As far as he was concerned, science had pounded the final nail into the coffin of religion, burying the need for God once and for all. Sadly, the one who had thought that God was dead was now dead himself. He'd had his chance. I can only hope that his eyes were somehow spiritually opened before they closed for the last time.

We have the German philosopher Friedrich Nietzsche to thank for announcing the supposed death of God. The sentiment was meant to communicate the idea that God is no longer necessary, as naturalism has rendered him irrelevant. To Nietzsche, it was time for humanity to give up the childish behavior of belief in God and march on toward naturalistic adulthood.

And yet, while Nietzsche may have been the first to articulate that God is dead, the same idea belonged to naturalistic philosophers of the past. As far back as the ancient world of Ionia, philosophers such as Thales of Miletus (620–546 BCE) sought to explain the world in rational terms—positing that water is the primary principle of the cosmos.[1] Then there was Anaximenes (586–526 BCE), who argued that air is the source of all things;[2]

and Heraclitus (540–480 BCE), who believed "the world is not to be identified with any particular substance, but rather with an ongoing process . . . of change," as "symbolized by fire."[3]

These thinkers sought to deliver naturalistic explanations for the cosmos without reference to God or other gods. And, of course, they were not alone. There were others like Democritus (460–370 BCE), with his atomic view, and the Roman poet and philosopher Lucretius (99–55 BCE), who poetically inked his own naturalistic worldview. However, these naturalistic accounts began to cool off with the rise of Christianity throughout the Roman Empire and its spread throughout Europe over the next several centuries.

But it wasn't until the Renaissance began to take shape in the fourteenth century of the modern era that a concentrated effort emerged to celebrate the world on naturalistic terms. Through humanism, the arts, and a wide range of scholarship, this move-ment aimed to show the potential of humanity to break free from the religious shackles of the past. This in turn carved the pathway to the Enlightenment, which offered an entirely new terrain of philosophical and scientific thought.

One luminary during the Enlightenment was Charles Darwin, whose release of *On the Origin of Species* in 1859 widened the ever-growing gap between religion and science, so much so that today people like Richard Dawkins can claim that "Darwin made it possible to be an intellectually fulfilled atheist."[4]

Nevertheless, contrary to the mantra that God is dead, the stats don't add up. According to David Baggett and Jerry L. Walls, "In many intellectual circles today, something like naturalism or materialism—the idea that the physical world exhausts reality— is the prevailing perspective, despite its minority standing in the larger culture and its relative scarcity throughout history."[5] When you consider how small this minority is—considerably less than 10 percent of Americans profess to be atheistic—it's astonishing how loud they've been. For all the so-called advancement that atheism has apparently brought us, it is unimpressive how miniscule its influence has been to persuade new converts.

Certainly, the New Atheists gained some acclaim for a time, especially in the last decade of the twentieth century; but like other movements that come and go, this one, too, has lost steam, and I suspect it won't be long before that brand of atheism is all but dead. If atheism is as sound a worldview as its adherents claim, why aren't more people joining their camp? I think it has a lot to do with its lack of appeal to potential adherents. Many people find it incomprehensible that the entire universe emerged *from* nothing and *by* nothing. Atheists come off as closed-minded when they so readily dismiss the conviction held by so many that God exists, and that he's also the source by which everything else exists, including humanity. Atheists present their faith in a godless universe as brilliant, enlightened, and unshackled from petty beliefs about all things supernatural. But it requires a certain intellectual hubris to hold this worldview. For starters, an atheist must deny every account of miracles, every account of people's religious experience, every account of answered prayer, every account of supernatural healing, and every account of divine providence. It takes a serious dose of chutzpah to deny every single account of divine action—chalking it up to the believer's delusions.

To me, that's what's incomprehensible.

Perhaps I can be more specific by offering five reasons for why I think such a large portion of our population refuses to believe that atheism has truly and finally buried God:

1. *Atheism struggles to objectively ground moral values and duties.* Some have attempted to objectively ground moral

values in the Platonic realm—in which, advocates claim, free-floating, abstract moral objects exist. What does that even mean? These so-called abstract moral objects are impersonal, which means that they can't be offended, nor can they call us to account for our failure to perform our moral duties. Why should anyone feel morally obligated to conform to a realm of abstract moral values—the existence of which most people have never even considered?

Other attempts have been made, such as Sam Harris's theory of human well-being, outlined in his book *The Moral Landscape*. But all of these atheistic ideas fail to supply the necessary foundation to ground objective moral values and duties the way that theism can. If we are to be morally obligated, there must be a qualified authority, such as a personal, good God who issues moral commands. Those commands in turn become our duties to obey, thereby morally obligating us to make good on them; in the event we don't, we are rendered guilty, regardless of our choice to agree or disagree.

2. *Atheism fails to offer its adherents a sense of ultimate meaning and purpose in life.* Not every atheist would agree, but there are certainly some who honestly recognize the bankruptcy of the atheistic worldview with its inability to provide an objective sense of meaning and purpose. For such nihilists, life is absurd. Christians would certainly concur that there is a meaninglessness to life without God. Atheists who aren't also nihilists seek to make the most of life . . . before they die. And then it's lights out. Forever.

3. *Atheism, as a worldview, is unequipped to lead people to a morally transformed life.* Though stories abound of people who have been morally transformed by Christ, it cannot be

said that someone's life has been morally transformed for the better by atheism. How many drug addicts, alcoholics, thieves, or adulterers have you met who exclaimed, "Once I learned that God didn't exist, it changed everything. I put the drugs and alcohol down, quit stealing, and went back to living faithfully with my spouse"? I'm guessing you haven't met any. Me either. In fact, I've never heard a single story from a committed atheist about how atheism had ethically transformed his or her life. That's because natural selection couldn't care less about ethics or morality—let alone transformation. Natural selection only cares about survival. In a world where many people feel as if survival is all that life amounts to, they want more of whatever they can get. But only Christianity offers "life . . . to the full."[6]

4. *The naturalistic view that the universe popped into existence out of nothing seems absurdly far-fetched to those who oppose a naturalistic explanation for the universe.* This is precisely why naturalism never appealed to me. It never got off the ground as a worldview for me because it seems so ridiculous to think that nothing took nothing and from it fashioned the universe. It still shocks me that anyone finds this theory compelling. Theism as an explanation for how the universe got here requires a lot less faith. God did it. Simple enough. It would serve us well as Christians to quit believing the charge that we are unintelligent or unthinking based on our belief in God and his creative genius. If any approach is naive, it's the one that suggests the universe came into existence uncaused, unplanned, and out of nothing.

5. *Atheism fails to offer hope beyond the grave.* Many people share an intuitive hunch that we are more than just our

bodies. Of all the humans to ever live, including those alive today, most have envisioned life after death. That's because we're not merely materialistic machines; we are embodied souls whose existence will outlast the grave. Atheism contends that humans are purely finite, physical beings. For the atheist, death is the final word. There is no hope beyond the grave.

Though I realize we shouldn't believe in something simply because it offers us hope of the afterlife, it seems to me that Christianity makes sense of this dualistic body/soul experience we intuit as human beings. If it's true, there's hope of being reunited with our believing loved ones—not to mention being fully and eternally united with God.

If that isn't the case . . . well, I'm reminded of Samuel Beckett's thirty-second play titled *Breath*, in which the curtain goes up to reveal a dimly lit stage replete with trash. The audience is treated to the sound of a massive, rasping inhale, followed by an equally massive, rasping exhale, and the curtain goes back down. Show's over. That's life. No wonder so few want to sign up for that vision.

I don't know what attracted Alan to atheism. He certainly left no room for the hope of an afterlife. To him, life was a sardonic joke, a short walk across a stage littered with rubbish. You live. You breathe. And then you die.

Some hope.

Some life.

Some death.

I wish Alan could have seen that Christianity offers something more. Something greater. Something truer. Something worth living and dying for. Some atheists say that Christianity doesn't make sense; but many more people would say it's atheism that doesn't make sense. And they'd be right. Unlike atheism, Christianity objectively grounds moral values and duties in a good, personal God; it offers a sense of ultimate meaning and purpose in life; it leads to a morally transformed life; it provides a more sensible explanation for the origin of the universe; and it offers believers hope beyond the grave. And if there's hope beyond the grave, here's something you can count on: God is *not* dead.

23

IS THERE RELIABLE EVIDENCE FOR GOD'S EXISTENCE?

I want atheism to be true and am made uneasy
by the fact that some of the most intelligent
and well-informed people I know are religious
believers. It isn't just that I don't believe in God
and, naturally, hope that I'm right in my belief.
It's that I hope there is no God! I don't want
there to be a God; I don't want the universe
to be like that.

THOMAS NAGEL

The story is told of the acclaimed nineteenth-century atheist philosopher Bertrand Russell, who was once asked what he would say if he were to stand before God at the judgment, only to be asked why he hadn't believed. Russell's response was simple: "Not enough evidence, God! Not enough evidence!"[1] I suppose French philosopher and mathematician Blaise Pascal was on to something when he supposedly quipped, "In faith there is enough light for those who want to believe and enough shadows to blind those who don't."[2] For some atheists, no matter how much light or evidence is presented, it will never be enough to persuade them. That's because their method of inquiry prohibits them from seeing the evidence. Many atheists ascribe to a theory known as methodological naturalism (MN), which is the epitome of a closed-minded methodology. MN can't appeal to divine agency as a form of evidence for causal explanations; instead, it explains things using only undirected physical or material causes. Consequently, the method serves as a Pascalian "shadow," blinding naturalists of their ability to see. No one captures the root of the problem of MN better than the late evolutionary biologist Richard Lewontin:

> Our willingness to accept scientific claims that are against common sense is the key to an understanding of the real struggle between science and the supernatural. We take the side of science in spite of the patent absurdity of some of its constructs, in spite of its failure to fulfill many of its extravagant promises of health and life, in spite of the tolerance of the scientific community for unsubstantiated just-so stories, because we have a prior commitment, a commitment to materialism. It is not that the methods and institutions of science somehow compel us to accept a material explanation of the phenomenal world, but, on the contrary, that we are forced by our a priori adherence to material causes to create an apparatus of investigation and a set of concepts that produce material explanations, no matter how counterintuitive, no matter how mystifying to the uninitiated. Moreover, that materialism is absolute, for we cannot allow a Divine Foot in the door.[3]

It's hard not to appreciate Lewontin's candor. I've often thought about how his fellow atheists must have resented him for giving theists a quote of such blistering honesty. It's ironic that theists are so often accused of ignorance, when we are the very ones willing to consider *all* the evidence, not only what methodological naturalism can produce. If anything, the mark of closed-mindedness is to not even consider alternative explanations beyond one's chosen method. It's the theists who are open-minded, for they haven't closed themselves off to weighing evidence beyond what naturalism has to offer—which is substantial.

Space limitations prohibit me from even scratching the surface of the multiple arguments for God's existence, but allow me to draw your attention to a few of the more helpful mainstream theories: cosmological, teleological (i.e., design), and moral.[4] These lines of reasoning are theistic in nature and aim to show that God is the creator, designer, and moral lawgiver. Such arguments can be used by any adherents to theism, such as Jews, Muslims, or Christians. To argue beyond theism—and, more specifically, *for* Christianity—requires another batch of arguments related to the reliability and trustworthiness of Scripture and in support of the historicity of the resurrection of Jesus Christ. What these three arguments demonstrate is a consistency with the God revealed in the Bible, who is indeed the Creator, Designer, and Moral Lawgiver.

The Cosmological Evidence for God's Existence

Let's first consider the cosmological argument. Don't let the fancy name scare you off. The structure of the argument is easy to grasp, and its most prominent version is the Kalam cosmological argument developed by William Lane Craig:

Premise 1: Everything that begins to exist has a cause.
Premise 2: The universe began to exist.
Conclusion: Therefore, the universe has a cause.

Premise 1 is the standard scholarly consensus today.[5] This premise is intuitively obvious: Things don't pop into existence from or out of nothing (*ex nihilo*). Coke machines, football stadiums, and Porsche 911s don't appear out of nowhere. Everything that begins to exist has a cause. Note the key word: *begins*. This is important because some people are quick to ask, "But who created God?" That question reveals a category mistake. It's like asking, "What does Beethoven's *Moonlight* Sonata taste like?" God didn't *begin* to exist, because God by definition is self-existent. He is a necessary being. If you were to provide an explanation for who created God, you'd then need to ask, "Who created *that* God?" and then, "Who created *that* God?" leading to an infinite regress. To help you grasp this concept, think of it like this: As a self-existent being, God is the uncaused cause of everything that exists. He is the *beginningless* Creator of all things.

Premise 2 is a little more involved, because there is both philosophical and scientific evidence to support it. Again, I'll offer just some food for thought.

We know scientifically that the universe had a beginning. Through the separate work of astronomers Georges Lemaître and Edwin Hubble, it was discovered that the universe is expanding. This was a phenomenal breakthrough in science, leading to later big-bang models beginning around 1948.

Another line of scientific evidence that provides confirmation of the second premise involves the laws of thermodynamics, which help us understand that there was an absolute beginning to the universe. Given Hubble's discoveries, combined with the laws of thermodynamics, the steady-state theory of the universe, with the premise of its existence throughout eternity, has been largely dismissed, leading to the conclusion that the universe had a cause. This cause was not random, nor did it come about through the agency of an ordinary being; rather, the genesis of the universe came about from one who is beyond space and time, immaterial, enormously powerful, and unimaginably intelligent. To generate space, time, and matter, the Creator would have needed to be spaceless, timeless, and immaterial. Moreover, the Creator would have to be enormously powerful and unimaginably intelligent to pull off this project of creating the universe with no material building blocks.

The Design Evidence for God's Existence

The second hypothesis is the teleological argument, or argument from design, which has been stunning in its ability to convince skeptics of God's existence. In fact, seeing good design and complexity in the world has arguably been one of the primary convincers for skeptics that God does indeed exist, as it has demonstrated that religious belief is more than just wishful thinking or a psychological crutch for the weak. It is, rather, rooted in well-thought-out arguments that demonstrate highly ordered and complex design. Though theists are often mocked for their superficial belief in a cosmic Creator, atheists must also dismiss the clear indication that the universe was constructed by an intelligent designer.

I loved going to Disneyland when I was growing up, and I especially enjoyed the bushes shaped like Disney characters at the entrance to the park. But I can assure you that I never once thought, *It's amazing how that bush randomly turned out to look like Mickey!* And I certainly never thought, *I should go to the gift shop and get some seeds to plant my very own Mickey bush.* No, it was obvious that a gardener had artistically sculpted the bush to look like our favorite cartoon mouse. Imagine how gullible I'd have to be to believe that Mickey seeds existed. And yet atheism doesn't provide even the *premise* of a seed to kickstart the design we see all around us. The only explanation that atheists can offer is that *nothingness* was the initial architect of the universe.

Here's something to think about. If David could utter, "The heavens declare the glory of God"[6] thousands of years before the scientific age, how much more should we be able to do so today, with all the new discoveries to which we are privy? For example, consider the anthropic principle, "a theory that focuses on human life as the main drive behind the existence of the universe."[7] The array of necessary conditions required for our existence is simply mind-boggling.

Take Jupiter, for instance, which serves as Earth's bodyguard, operating like a cosmic vacuum cleaner, protecting us from being wiped out by objects such as comets and asteroids. Then there is our proximity to the sun. If we were a hairbreadth closer (in cosmic dimensions), our planet would melt. A hairbreadth further away and we'd freeze. These are just a few of the many, many complex and incredibly precise parameters necessary for our existence.[8]

Another mind-blowing discovery has been human DNA, which provides strong evidence of intelligent design. The vast amount of information contained in our DNA is simply stunning. Our bodies contain trillions of incredibly sophisticated DNA-infused cells, all working together to help us function. Human physiology, consciousness, and personality cannot be explained as the mere outcome of random forces. We have an intelligent designer to thank for that.

The Moral Evidence for God's Existence

Of all the arguments for God's existence, the moral argument is my personal favorite because it really seems to hit home for people. It does more than resonate intellectually; it also offers a powerful emotional punch—disrupting the conscience by convincing people of their guilt before God. Moving beyond personal value judgments and moral relativism, this argument objectively grounds the moral law in God's supremely good nature.

In his book *Mere Christianity*, C. S. Lewis writes, "You find out more about God from the Moral Law than from the universe in general just as you find out more about a man by listening to his conversation than by looking at a house he has built."[9] A person with a lively conscience might well agree.

In his letter to the Romans, Paul tells his readers that God has written his moral law on our hearts, regardless of whether we believe in him:

> Indeed, when Gentiles, who do not have the law, do
> by nature things required by the law, they are a law for
> themselves, even though they do not have the law. They
> show that the requirements of the law are written on their
> hearts, their consciences also bearing witness, and their
> thoughts sometimes accusing them and at other times
> even defending them.[10]

When I was a new believer, these verses blew me away because they corresponded perfectly with my own experience before I committed my life to Christ. If there was one emotion, besides anxiety, with which I was all too familiar as a young man, it was guilt. I can still envision myself standing miserably in my parents' laundry room, stunned by heart-wrenching guilt over a decision I had made. And yet there I was, asking God to forgive me. I didn't even know who God was, but I certainly suspected I was no stranger to him. Upon reflection, I recognize that my feelings of guilt were good, and productive, like a check-engine light revealing that something was broken within me and needed repair.

The topic of guilt has long fascinated me—so much so that I took the topic all the way into a second doctoral program, where I developed a unique version of the moral argument from guilt. Obviously, as with the other arguments, there are many versions. Typically, moral arguments begin with a particular aspect of morality, such as conscience, law, shame, moral values and duties, obligation, or, as in my case, guilt. The argument proceeds to show that God's existence is the best objective explanation to account for these features of morality.[11] In my doctoral thesis, I argue from moral guilt to show how it points to God's existence—including five objective attributes of God that can be discovered from our guilt; namely, that he is personal, all-knowing, good, a moral law-giver, and fit to hold us accountable.[12]

The Power of a Transformed Life

I hope you don't feel overwhelmed by all this information. Though these arguments are very helpful for eliminating some of the barriers that often prevent unbelievers from seeing the truth, we are wise not to underestimate the simple power of living transformed lives before our unbelieving friends. A life fully devoted to Christ can serve as a powerful argument for God's existence, just as a sloppily lived life can have an adverse effect.[13]

As Christians, we need to be aware that people are paying attention, and that how we live matters. I saw this firsthand years ago with an atheist I worked with at the Ritz Carlton. He was an extremely likable guy, but he didn't hesitate to boast about his atheism. When we first met, he couldn't have cared less about Christianity. He simply wasn't interested. But as we cultivated a friendship, he became willing to at least hear me out—though I didn't have any apologetic arguments for God's existence. Fortunately, that didn't prevent God from using me.

What I did have was a transformed life, and that proved to be a powerful witness. It certainly caught my friend's attention. I remember him telling me that he had been watching the way I lived, and that he was drawn to the change that had taken place in my life—especially to the evident sense of purpose I now had. I'll never forget the time he decided to tag along with me to church for Easter Sunday, and how it seemed as if the message had been handcrafted specifically for him.

It was shocking enough that he came to church with me, but I was completely unprepared for my atheist friend to commit his life to Christ. And this was no whimsical decision on his part. From that point forward, his previous atheistic stance was dead history. It was now my turn to watch his life transform before my very eyes, and I even had the privilege of baptizing him.

So be encouraged. You may not know a single philosophical argument for God's existence. Neither did I. Just as God used me to reach an atheist for Christ, he can use you, too. In fact, he'll be more than happy to give you an opportunity to serve as a living apologetic before a watching world.

24

HOW CAN PEOPLE BELIEVE IN MIRACLES TODAY?

Western Christians have absorbed more of a secular worldview than we like to admit, and many of them find miracle stories hard to believe or even embarrassing. . . . The secularization of American culture, especially of cultural elites like university professors, those in the media and entertainment industry, and many politicians, has led to widespread ridicule toward and skepticism about all things supernatural.

J. P. MORELAND

"It's a miracle you're alive. God must have something special in store for you, Bobby." That's what my mother told me after I survived what could have been a fatal car accident during my senior year of high school. It happened one night as I was speeding through the Santa Cruz Mountains on my way to the beach. You would've thought I was Mario Andretti. As I foolishly ripped around a tight curve going fifty-plus, I lost control and hit another car head-on. That was bad enough, but if I hadn't struck the other driver, I would have driven directly off a cliff.

It was a horrific night. I hurriedly got my liquor out of the car and threw it down the hill before the ambulance and police arrived. I knew I was in trouble, and I panicked when I heard the loud screams of the man in the other car. When the ambulance arrived, they had to saw him out of the car and rush him down the mountain to a medevac helicopter that took him to the hospital. Amazingly, my passengers and I were okay, despite a few bangs and bruises.

The injured driver later sued my parents for the physical damage he suffered as the result of my stupidity, and I lost my driver's license for six months. Before leaving that night for the beach, I had laid down a blanket in the back seat of my car, which prevented my two friends from accessing their lap belts. The force of the impact was so powerful that the doctor said, "It's a good thing they didn't have their seat belts on; had they been on, the impact would have severed them in half."

Not surprisingly, that was a lot to digest. And it wasn't my first accident. I had taken my old Suzuki Samurai off a jump and put it on its side. I'd been hit by an eighteen-wheeler on the freeway and totaled my grandfather's car. And there'd been other dingers as well. Still, the wreck that night was sobering, to say the least.

But was it really a *miracle* I was alive?

Well, I guess it all depends on how you define a miracle. If you consider a miracle an act by which God intervenes to disrupt normal processes in the natural world, then it's certainly possible that God somehow intervened supernaturally to save our lives that night. But how could we ever know, after the fact, that he had done so? The lack of objective quantifiability or measurable verification becomes the issue with defining miracles too broadly. Though I'm perfectly content to view the outcome of that accident as a miracle, there have been other instances in which the term was clearly abused:

"It's a miracle I got that parking spot."

"It's a miracle I woke up on time."

"It's a miracle I passed that test."

You get the point.

The word *miracle* loses its definition if practically any incident with an unexpectedly positive outcome can qualify as one. But if we're talking about the parting of the Red Sea, the feeding of the five thousand, or the sun standing still, I think we would all agree those were bona fide miracles. In fact, those types of events are so unquestionably miraculous that skeptics tend to deny them altogether. That's because it's nearly impossible to account for them on exclusively naturalistic terms—though critics over the years have certainly tried. For the naturalist, it's easier to deny a miraculous occurrence altogether than attempt to offer a naturalistic explanation. Obviously, we don't want to call everything a miracle, but neither should we deny that miracles can happen.

The crux of believing or disbelieving in miracles comes down to our worldview. Various worldviews can fall under the umbrella of naturalism or supernaturalism, but for the sake of simplicity, let's consider naturalism as the atheistic view, and supernaturalism as the theistic view.

From a naturalistic perspective, the universe is a closed box; nothing exists beyond or outside of it. Thus, the only place to find explanations for the origin of the cosmos and everything that happens there is inside the box. And because the box is all that exists, naturalism precludes the possibility of miracles.

Naturalists, therefore, have a dyed-in-the-wool commitment to reject every fact that might serve to substantiate a miracle. Like flat-earthers denying that the earth is spherical, despite the evidence, naturalists are blinded by their worldview from seeing the truth about miracles.

David Hume, the eighteenth-century Scottish philosopher, was notorious for his outright rejection of miracles. He denied the possibility of miracles to the point of stating that it would be unreasonable under any circumstance to believe in them, regardless of the strength of the evidence. For Hume, miracles would be a violation of the laws of nature—whereas, for Christians, they are evidence of God's intervening *within* the laws of nature.

Think of it this way: If I were walking beneath a lemon tree and caught a lemon that was falling, I wouldn't have violated the law of gravity; I would have simply intervened in the life of the lemon by catching it before it could hit the ground. Or bounce off my head.

If God created the universe, certainly he can intervene in the world he created; besides, he instituted the very laws of nature that seemingly blind the naturalist from recognizing him. At the core, naturalists don't have a problem with believing in miracles but with believing in God. Once God is able to open the box, miracles become possible.

We could argue the point in this way:

Premise 1: If God exists, miracles are possible.
Premise 2: God exists.
Conclusion: Therefore, miracles are possible.

Obviously, the naturalist would reject the second premise and therefore reject the conclusion. But as we saw in the previous chapter, there are compelling arguments that establish the likelihood of God's existence. That said, any conversation with a naturalist about miracles will likely prove fruitless unless and until belief in God is first established. But if such a discussion takes place, it can be helpful for believers to have a grasp of the way miracles worked in the Bible. They were *rare* acts of God to confirm his messengers as his authentic representatives. In his book *Stealing from God*, apologist Frank Turek sets the record straight by putting the situation in perspective:

Even in the Bible miracles are relatively rare. There are approximately 250 occurrences of miracles in the Bible. From Abraham to the apostles is about 2,000 years. If you were to spread those miracles out evenly, there would be one miracle every eight years (and even less frequent for miracles done before crowds). Of course, miracles did not occur every eight years—they occurred in bunches. . . . The main point is that miracles are *still* rare even in the Bible. Most events in the Bible were natural, regular events like they are today, which enabled miracles to stand out when they occurred.

Since the primary purpose of miracles is to confirm new revelation, and since miracles have to be rare to have their intended effect, it's no wonder that miracles are not as frequent today.[1]

The miracles recorded in Scripture, though sprinkled in various spots throughout the text, were primarily captured during three pivotal periods: during the times of Moses and Joshua, Elijah and Elisha, and Jesus and the apostles. The miracles helped to confirm these leaders as God's messengers. When we consider the lengthy time gaps between the Old Testament leaders and prophets and the coming of Jesus, we can see just how sparse miraculous intervention was in the overall redemptive plan of God.

Between the times of Joshua and Elijah, there was a gap of more than five hundred years; and the gap between Elisha and Jesus was well over eight hundred years. Taken together, these three periods represent the law, the prophets, and the inauguration of the New Covenant. As we have noted, it appears that there was a heightening of the incidence of miraculous events during these pivotal periods. In addition to these three stages, we know from

Scripture—especially from the book of Revelation—that there will be a fourth and final period of miracles during the end times.

Christians who believe in miracles are not asserting that they happen all the time; if they did, they would no longer be classified as miracles. Miracles, by their very nature, are irregular, supernatural occurrences. Christians who believe in miracles aren't even claiming that they've witnessed one; rather, they're simply contending that miracles *can* happen, *have* happened, and *will* happen. We make that assertion on the basis of our belief in an all-powerful God. If God exists, miracles are possible.

As Christians, we can't deny miracles. Christianity is a miracle-believing religion. It always has been and always will be. If you're skeptical about miracles, don't stress yourself by trying to embrace the approximately 250 reported miracles in the Bible; rather, seek to come to terms with the first miracle of creation described in the very first verse of the Bible: "In the beginning, God created the heavens and the earth."[2] And come to grips with the resurrection of Jesus Christ.[3]

The apostle Paul was so confident about the Resurrection that he said, "If Christ has not been raised, our preaching is useless and so is your faith."[4] In other words, if the reported miracle of Christ's resurrection is false, then Christianity is also false and we've been duped. But the opposite is also true. If Jesus did rise from the grave, then this was unquestionably a miracle, on a level all its own. This is wholly unlike my mom saying, "It's a miracle you're alive, Bobby." Because, unlike Jesus, I never died. If Jesus died only to rise again, there is no other option but to recognize this rising as a miracle. And the implication is this: If the miracle of the Resurrection is true, then Christianity is also true.

25

DID JESUS *REALLY* RISE FROM THE DEAD?

We should be taking steps to celebrate Easter
in creative new ways.... This is our greatest
festival.... Take Easter away, and you don't have
a New Testament; you don't have a Christianity;
as Paul says, you are still in your sins.

N. T. WRIGHT

Following the first Easter Sunday, rumors quickly spread to deny
Christ's resurrection. It's easy to understand why. The critics knew
that if they could debunk the Resurrection, Christianity would
crumble. And they weren't wrong about that. As the apostle Paul
later observed, "If Christ has not been raised, your faith is futile
and you are still in your sins."[1] The problem for atheists and others
who don't believe in Jesus is that none of the objections raised by
skeptics have been able to explain away the Resurrection. That's
because their claims are flimsy attempts to discredit the eyewitness
accounts. For a brief sampling, here are three such theories:

1. *Some skeptics claimed that Jesus' body was stolen.* This was
   the first theory to emerge in an attempt to deny Christ's

resurrection. But think about it: If Jesus' body had been stolen, don't you think the thieves would have brought it forward to disprove the disciples' claim that Jesus was alive? And if the disciples had stolen the body, do you really think they would have been willing to die to perpetuate a hoax? In the words of the late Paul E. Little, former director of evangelism for InterVarsity, "Men will die for what they *believe* to be true, though it may actually be false. They do not, however, die for what they *know* is a lie."[2]

Charles Colson, who spent time in prison for his role in the Watergate scandal, was convinced that the Resurrection is a fact. Why?

> Because twelve men testified they had seen Jesus raised from the dead, and then they proclaimed that truth for forty years, never once denying it. Everyone was beaten, tortured, stoned, and put in prison. They would not have endured that if it weren't true. Watergate embroiled twelve of the most powerful men in the world and they couldn't keep a lie for three weeks. You're telling me twelve apostles could keep a lie for forty years? Absolutely impossible.[3]

2. *Some skeptics claimed that people were hallucinating.* This one seems a bit far-fetched and desperate, don't you think? Perhaps one could make such an argument if there were one or two random encounters. But Jesus appeared to his disciples on several occasions—one of which included five hundred people at once.[4] To think that a crowd that large collectively hallucinated the resurrected Christ is absurd.

Moreover, it's hard to attribute to hallucinations and imaginations the radical life change experienced by Saul of Tarsus following his encounter with Jesus on the Damascus Road, or the transformation of Jesus' half-brother James, who did not at first believe in him. And then there's Thomas, who insisted on touching the risen Jesus before he could believe; and Peter, who likely would have carried to his grave the shame of having denied Jesus if he had not encountered the resurrected Christ and been reinstated to fellowship with him.[5]

3. *Some skeptics claimed that Jesus merely passed out.* This is known as the "swoon theory," a view popularized in the eighteenth century that Jesus didn't actually die on the cross, but merely passed out. To cast aspersions on the Resurrection, adherents to the swoon theory contend that after Jesus was mistaken for dead and placed in the tomb, he regained consciousness, extricated himself from seventy-five pounds of spice-infused burial cloths, then rolled away the stone at the mouth of the tomb and said, "Check it out, folks. I'm alive." All this after being severely scourged, having his hands and feet nailed to a cross, his head punctured by a crown of thorns, and his side pierced by Roman soldiers tasked with taking his life? I don't think so. They made sure he was good and dead before they took him down off the cross.

These lame attempts (and there have been others) to explain away the Resurrection show that it's easier—and, frankly, more *rational*—to simply believe the truth: *Jesus rose from the dead.*

During my extended season of doubt, I knew I had to come to terms with the Resurrection. If I could explain it away, then I should renounce Christianity and walk away from it all. But if I *couldn't*, then I had better stay put. It's not that I *wanted* to explain it away, but I wanted to make sure I was giving my life to the truth as best as I could determine.

Regarding evidence in support of the Resurrection, here are four lines of reasoning that I couldn't explain away:

1. *Prophecy.* The prophecies about the life, death, and resurrection of Jesus are so precise that the only argument skeptics can muster is that the authors must have added material after the fact to make it seem more convincing. But that's a pretty weak point. Some of the prophecies were given seven hundred to a thousand years prior to their fulfillment. And even apart from Old Testament passages, such as Psalm 16:9-10 and Isaiah 53:11 that foreshadow Christ's resurrection, Jesus himself is recorded in all four Gospels saying that he was going to die and rise again in three days.[6] A simple reading of his life in the Gospels shows that Jesus was in total control of the events unfolding around him. Never has anyone been so exact in predicting the outcome of events as Jesus was. The apostle Paul leveraged his knowledge of Scripture to affirm the validity of the Resurrection, drawing on an early Christian confession in his first letter to the Corinthians: "For I delivered to you as of first importance what I also received: that Christ died for our sins in accordance with the Scriptures, that he was buried, that he was raised on the third day in accordance with the Scriptures."[7]

2. *The empty tomb.* No one was ever able to produce the body of Jesus, despite their claims that the body had been stolen.

But if someone had taken the body, they most certainly would have called the disciples' bluff for claiming that Jesus had risen from the dead. Think about all the drama surrounding his death. He was buried in the private tomb of a prominent citizen, Joseph of Arimathea, and the tomb was guarded by a crew of Roman soldiers put there precisely to prevent anyone from stealing the body. Those soldiers served under penalty of death for failing to complete their mission. Nevertheless, despite the safeguards put in place to ensure that Christ's body remained sealed in the grave, the stone was rolled away, and his body disappeared without its burial wrappings, and without a trace—except of course for those post-Resurrection appearances of the living Jesus recorded in the New Testament.

3. *Post-Resurrection appearances.* In Acts 1:3, Luke writes, "After his suffering, he presented himself to them and gave many convincing proofs that he was alive. He appeared to them over a period of forty days and spoke about the kingdom of God." Jesus appeared first to women, which is quite significant given that the testimony of a woman in the first century was considered less than credible. If the disciples were trying to fake a resurrection, and if the Gospel writers were fabricating their stories, they certainly wouldn't have chosen women to be the first eyewitnesses. Including that fact underscores their integrity in recording what happened.

Jesus also appeared to other disciples on several occasions, including Peter, Thomas, James, Paul, and more than five hundred people at one time.[8] These appearances were meant to validate Christ's resurrection. Not only was his body missing from the tomb, but he was seen alive by many, many eyewitnesses.

4. *Transformative life change.* This is a biggie. Before the Resurrection, the disciples could hardly follow Jesus without arguing with one another and scratching their heads at what Jesus said and did. But after the Resurrection, they were ready to suffer and even die, if necessary, to spread the gospel. Characters like Peter, Paul, Thomas, and James all had their lives transformed by encountering the resurrected Jesus. How do you explain Paul's radical life change apart from the Resurrection? I mean, here was a guy with a one-track mind to persecute Christians, and while traveling with letters in hand to arrest even more, he himself was arrested—by Jesus himself, on the road to Damascus. Paul went on to plant churches and to write more letters that wound up in the New Testament than any other author. Eventually he died a martyr's death in Rome, under Nero, for his unstoppable belief in Christ.

The church never would have gotten off the ground apart from the Resurrection. But with the power of the Resurrection, many lives would forever be changed—including mine.

WHY CHRISTIANITY STILL MAKES SENSE TO ME

I believe in Christianity as I believe that the Sun has risen, not only because I see it, but because by it I see everything else.

C. S. LEWIS

I began this book by sharing my struggle to make sense of Christianity, while also sharing some of the factors that contributed to my doubts. Now, as I wrap things up, I'd like to share why Christianity *still* makes sense to me. It's not that I don't still have questions. I do. Nor is it that everything makes sense to me as a Christian. It doesn't. As Christians, we are far removed from the context in which the Bible was written, so it makes sense that some things won't make sense. In those instances, I try to place myself in the cultural context in which the Bible was written and remember that God was meeting people where they were to bring them to where he is. Our wise and gracious God meets people on their own turf, according to their own worldviews, and then brings them to his turf to give them his view of the world.

It's cultural snobbery to dismiss the parts of the Bible we can't relate to, as if our culture is the enlightened one that has finally figured it all out. It doesn't take a genius to realize that our culture has its own weird ways. In these final few pages, I want to share how my faith remained intact after having been hammered for years by doubt. Though I don't intend to suggest a magic formula, I do want to offer some hope to fellow doubters. As I've reflected on my journey through doubt, there are four primary reasons Christianity still makes sense to me, . . . and there is one ultimate key that led me out of the maze of doubt.

Four Primary Reasons Christianity Still Makes Sense to Me

1. *Even if I tried, I couldn't explain away the overwhelming evidence for the resurrection of Jesus Christ.* As a believer, I knew the Resurrection was the linchpin of Christianity. As previously noted, Paul the apostle is unequivocal about this: "If Christ has not been raised, your faith is futile; you are still in your sins."[1] This is Paul's way of saying, "Hey, if the Resurrection can be explained away because it didn't happen, then you're wasting your time playing church. If the Resurrection isn't true, then neither is Christianity." That's a truly sobering and life-shattering claim.

   During my period of doubt, I took Paul at his word. If the Resurrection truly is the linchpin of Christianity, I wanted to see whether it could be removed. As a Christian apologist, I was already familiar with the various arguments for and against the Resurrection, but now I wanted to take Paul to task to see whether I could explain it away. And as I explained in the previous chapter, I couldn't. The evidence for it is so overwhelmingly powerful in comparison to the desperate arguments against it that anything I sought to add to the mix was simply unable to move the needle. The linchpin remained intact.

This was crucial for me in my despair, because belief in the resurrection of Jesus Christ opened a way to quiet my other doubts. I reasoned as follows: If Jesus really rose from the dead, then he really did die. If he really did die, then he really did live. And while he was alive, he prophesied that he was going to die and rise again. Which he did, if you're following my train of reasoning. Beyond that, he confirmed the reliability of the Old Testament, promising the disciples that the Holy Spirit would come and lead them into all truth. For me, this made all the difference. From there, I was able to reason that if Jesus validated the trustworthiness of the Old Testament during his first coming, doesn't it make sense that he will validate the trustworthiness of the New Testament at his second appearance?

Do you see what I am saying? The Resurrection was the game changer. All the particulars of the Bible I worried about could be rolled back into the question of whether Jesus rose from the dead. And if the Old Testament was good enough for Jesus, who is all-knowing, then it would certainly be good enough for me.

2. *In the face of overwhelming doubts, I couldn't dismiss the assurance provided by the inner witness of the Holy Spirit.* In his letter to the Romans, Paul reminds his readers, "The Spirit himself testifies with our spirit that we are God's children."[2] Regardless of what anyone believes, we have this

in common: No one on earth is omniscient. We're all in the same boat. Everyone commits to a worldview position without exhaustively validating and codifying their beliefs. Imagine how overwhelming such an endeavor would be. To have to identify and articulate everything about your developing worldview before finally committing to it would be impossible. The good news for us as Christians is that we don't have to know everything about Christianity to have an assurance that it's true. That's because God has provided a witness, through the Holy Spirit, to assure us of our faith.

I remember hearing the great Christian philosopher Alvin Plantinga share an encouraging illustration of how Christians can be assured of the veracity of their faith, even though we may not be able to convince our critics.

Plantinga asked us to imagine standing before a court of law, accused of a crime we did not commit—though, for all practical purposes, the stack of evidence appears to weigh heavily against us. We *look* guilty. Plantinga pointed out that, if we didn't commit the crime, we would still be justified to believe in our own innocence, even though we "looked" guilty, and even though we can't explain away the evidence against us.

Plantinga used this illustration to establish that we don't need to know how to answer every question the critics might raise in order to have assurance of our Christian faith, because our belief is warranted through the inner witness of the Holy Spirit, who assures us of the truthfulness of Christianity, even in the presence of those who may try to convince us otherwise. This is encouraging. There are plenty of Christians who will never have the time or inclination to track down answers to all the questions the world may throw their way; and yet, as believers, they can still enjoy the assurance that Christianity is authentic and unimpeachable through the inner witness of God's Holy Spirit.

The witness of the Holy Spirit is not necessarily experienced as a warm and fuzzy feeling—it's more like a settled conviction that Christianity is true. To be honest, this was hard for me, because during my season of doubt my conviction wasn't all that settled. At times my soul felt hollow, absent from God, and in sheer agony. I feared I had gotten it all wrong. But through it all, God never let me escape his love . . . even when I couldn't feel it, even when his presence wasn't palpable. He eventually saw me through.

If you're in that place, tormented by doubt, stay the course, my friend. Refuse to panic when you don't feel God's presence or when you lack a sense of assurance. Many Christians have endured long seasons of feeling godforsaken, confused, and abandoned, wondering where God has gone. Working through this process took *years* for me; but in his time, the God of light met me again in my dark night, and once again I could tangibly sense both his presence and the conviction that Christianity and its claims are indeed valid. Upon reflection, I recognized that this assurance had been there all along, even when I couldn't sense it, and God had carried me through. And for that I'm thankful.

3. *I couldn't discount past spiritual encounters, such as God's providential leading and his overwhelming precision in answering specific prayers.* I've often said to those who doubt, "When you can't see through the windshield, look through the

rearview mirror at God's faithfulness." There were times when I couldn't see the road in front of me. It felt like I could crash at any moment and wipe out into apostasy. I wish I could say I never panicked, but that would be a lie. I can worry with the best of them. But during my dark night, I learned to develop a positive mindset that pulled me out of my spiritual negativity. I did this by recounting God's past faithfulness to me. This was very helpful. Whenever I wondered whether I would fall away, I'd reflect and remember the various evidences I couldn't deny. Spiritual encounters. Providential leading. And precise answers to targeted prayers. There had been too many clear examples of God's faithfulness for me to simply explain them away.

4. *I could not ignore the overall strength of the cumulative case for Christianity, compared to the evidence for other belief options.* As I mentioned above, my being a Christian doesn't mean that everything about the Christian faith makes sense to me; but when I considered the cumulative case for Christianity, as compared to the evidence for other worldviews, Christianity made far greater sense.

Fast-forward to today. The longer I have walked with Christ, the more I've grown to deeply appreciate the fully orbed worldview of Christianity. As a comprehensive view of reality, the Christian faith must be viewed as a whole, not in bits and pieces. By examining the various snapshots taken together, we can see the fuller picture of Christianity. While each piece of evidence for the faith, considered on its own merits, can strengthen our confidence, that's nothing compared to the confidence we gain when we consider the larger cumulative case.

For me to step back, after years of study, and see how God used my doubts to get me to chase down answers, all the while strengthening me as a Christian apologist, and eventually escorting me out of the dark night of doubt to see the brilliance of the fuller picture of Christianity, was deeply meaningful and eye-opening. No longer am I tormented by doubt. Today I stand in awe of the colorful, complete picture of Christianity compared to all the incomplete worldviews on offer. From my vantage point, Christianity is a home run, and every other worldview is like a bunt in comparison. Christianity has what it takes to bring us across home plate.

The Ultimate Key to Escaping the Maze of Doubt

Even though I had thought through the above four reasons very carefully, it wasn't until I discovered the ultimate key that I was able to escape the dark cave of doubt. The irony of my entire journey was that I finally found my way out of the maze in much the same way I had found Christianity in the first place. Learning to have faith like a child once again. That was the key that unlocked the door for me to walk out of my prison. Perhaps you wish the answer were more sophisticated. More erudite. More complex. But it wasn't—at least not for me. Though each of the points addressed above proved helpful, when all was said and done it was the return to a childlike trust that led me to the final door . . . and placed in my hand the key that enabled me to exit at last from the maze of confusion.

I had lost myself along the way by reducing my walk with Christ to an endless Q&A session. I needed to come to the end of my continuous quest for omniscience. God had been faithful to me, and now it was time for me to remain faithful to him. Instead of trying to get all my questions answered before I could feel okay again, I had to learn to be okay with some unanswered questions.

We can't allow ourselves to fall into a crisis of faith every time something, or someone, challenges our beliefs. I was done with that. There had to be something more than pure knowledge to set me straight. And there was. But the answer I needed wasn't another book, another lecture, or another class. No, what I needed was to relearn simple, childlike trust in God. The answer was *relational*, not intellectual. It was learning to abide, to trust, and to rest in Jesus.

So, with unconditional and unquestioning faith, I humbled myself and cast myself into his arms. This wasn't a one-time mystical encounter; it became a way of life. As adult believers, we must never forget what Jesus said about children: "Truly I tell you, anyone who will not receive the kingdom of God like a little child will never enter it."[3] We all know it. There's something so refreshing about a child's ability to trust. And that's exactly what I had lost: the simplicity of uncompromising faith. Through my doubts, my walk with Christ had become so *complicated*; but by learning to simply trust once again, I was able to spiritually *rest*. The good news is that you can too.

I realize my answer won't satisfy the ardent skeptic. I don't expect it to. This is the part of the equation that I can't transfer from me to you. It's the stuff Christianity is made of: *simple trust*. And yet it's also the part that resonates with any true believer. We share the common bond of being part of something bigger than ourselves. The inner sense that we *belong* to Jesus. That we are sealed with the Holy Spirit, even when we feel as if we have lost our way.

For us as Christians, the way home never changes. It's found through simple, unsophisticated, guileless trust in Jesus. The way home is relational. Jesus is the Good Shepherd who guides us and leads us home. Beyond that, he said, "I am the *gate*; whoever enters through me will be saved."[4] To get out of the dark labyrinth of doubt, I had to find the exit. That gate was Jesus. He was also the key that turned the knob to set me free at last. He has always been the key. And he always will be.

A WAY FORWARD FOR THE CHURCH

A movement that cannot or will not draw boundaries, or that allows the modern cultural fear of exclusion to set its theological agenda, is doomed to lose its doctrinal identity. Once it does, it will drift from whatever moorings it may have had in historic Christianity.

CARL R. TRUEMAN

Unless I am convicted by Scripture and plain reason—I do not accept the authority of popes and councils, for they have contradicted each other—my conscience is captive to the Word of God. I cannot and I will not recant anything, for to go against conscience is neither right nor safe. God help me. Amen.

MARTIN LUTHER

In this afterword, I will be putting on my pastoral hat and offering a way forward for the church during these challenging times. But first I must lay a little more groundwork. If we're to find our way forward, we must first understand the times in which we live. That understanding will help us develop a missional mindset, which in turn could lead to a new reformation within the church.

On a recent visit to Starbucks with my wife, Heather, we were served by a young woman whose name tag listed her pronoun preferences as they/them. After taking my order, they said, "It'll be right up, sir." I'm not sure why they assumed I was a man, but I took no offense. I *am* a man. But I do find it ironic that some champions of the pronoun discussion are guilty of breaking their own rules—assuming the obvious about others who don't wear their preferences on a name tag.

Out of genuine curiosity, I struck up a friendly conversation with the barista and said, "I noticed you called me 'sir.' And typically, we use *sir* or *ma'am* for male or female adults. But what does 'they/them' use for a title?"

"For the nonbinary person," the barista replied, "it's Mx or M. Or some people might prefer Misc."

I wish I could say that was helpful, but it wasn't. If anything, I found myself even more confused by the hijacking of the English language in our culture today.

As Heather and I left the Starbucks that day, we both felt overwhelmed by how much our country has changed. I wish I could say that gender obsession is our culture's only problem. Not by a mile.

A systematic dismantling of the United States of America is taking place right before our eyes, and the so-called postmodern deconstructionists are just getting started with their project to dismantle the past. By co-opting the Marxist idea of the bourgeoisie and proletariat and recasting these terms under the guise of oppressed and oppressor, these radical activists are seeking to bring about a revolution through an assortment of critical theories. Whether it's queer theory, gender theory, literary theory, critical race theory, post-colonial theory, or something else, these new revolutionaries are leveraging a hermeneutic of *suspicion* to root out every hint of oppression—past or present, real or imagined—to consign it to the dustbin of American history.

Other characteristics of the postmodern mindset is the tendency to be anti-rationalist, anti-realist, anti-objectivity, anti-universal, anti-modernity, anti-power structure (except their own, of course), anti-individual, and anti-capitalist, not to mention a morally relativistic commitment to obliterate any vestige of reason left over from the Age of Enlightenment that dominated the seventeenth and eighteenth centuries in Europe. With the rhetorical savvy of the ancient Greek sophists, some culture warriors have drunk from the fountain of Machiavelli and will say or do whatever it takes to erect their new world order. The message is clear: comply or be canceled. Cooperate or we're coming after you. And, oh, by the way, once the power is ours in full, use of force to gain compliance will not be out of the question. You can see this worldview at work in their militant secularism.

If modernism was overly rational, then postmodernism is decidedly irrational. René Descartes, often referred to as the father of modern philosophy, is perhaps best known for the principle he articulated during a time of his own deconstruction: *Cogito, ergo sum* (I think, therefore I am). If *thinking* reigned supreme under the umbrella of modernism, then *feeling* reigns supreme under postmodernism. Can you see it? The postmodernist says, "If you're a woman and you feel like a they/them, then you are. If you're a man and you feel like you're a woman, then you are." Admittedly, today's version of postmodernism looks different from its initial version with its intellectual musings. Today's version is *applied* postmodernism. Activism is the name of the game under the guise of social justice. And critical theory is the rule they follow. By attaching their postmodern worldview to Marxist principles of overthrow, they've found a way to execute their vision.

The deconstruction has begun, and I fear we're just getting started. It's no secret. The cultural zeitgeist in America has radically changed as we've officially entered a new epoch that's unfolding before our eyes. We don't have a name for it yet, but it's unmistakable that we are in the midst of a cultural revolution that will one day acquire a name like every other revolution before it, such as the Age of Enlightenment, the Industrial Age, or the Renaissance. Perhaps ours will be called the Moral Revolution, but that's for future historians to figure out after all the dust has settled from the deconstruction and reconstruction now underway.

At this point we can't quite label it, but we certainly feel it. And I'm afraid this massive cultural earthquake has not yet reached its peak. It appears the deconstructionists are just getting started and have no intention of letting up any time soon. But one day, after the quake and the aftershocks settle down, we'll have a better understanding of what this revolution entailed and what became of America because of it.

As great as the influence of postmodern deconstructionism is, it isn't the only influence contributing to the revolution. In the next section, we will consider the importance of developing a missional mindset in order to have a positive impact on our culture.

Developing a Missional Mindset

During an episode of *Pastors' Perspective*, a questioner called in who was curious about how Christians can engage the culture without compromising our convictions in the process. At that point my cohost, Brian Brodersen, said to me, "Bobby, don't you think if we are going to reach this culture, we are going to have to rethink our methods of outreach, instead of just hanging on to methods that worked in an old America?" Bingo. Brian hit the nail on the head: We must *contextualize* the gospel, the same way a missionary would when heading off to a foreign culture.

American culture is not the same as it once was. Once upon a time, most people in America adhered to values similar to those of the church, but that time is now ancient history. The methods we used to reach America in the 1980s, 1990s, and early 2000s need an update. If we hope to be effective, we must adopt a *missionary mindset* in the church. Part of the problem is that many people in the church haven't been taught to *think*. They want to *feel* something or *do* something, which is all well and good, but not at the expense of thinking and being prepared to "give an answer . . . for the hope" we have.[1] We must *think* for the sake of the Great Commission. If we want to know how to connect the gospel to our culture, we must equip people to take a missional approach in their communities—a way to think about the world we live in and how best to engage it. I've developed a list to kick-start the process. It's by no means exhaustive, but it can get you started in the right direction.

1. Churches with a missional mindset help believers understand the belief landscape.

This is crucial. Effective missionaries know the importance of learning the culture *before* setting out to reach it. Before I planted my first church in 2004, I attended a church-planting leadership residency that clearly taught the principle of learning the culture. To prepare us before we arrived on scene, the program required us to make twenty-five observations about specific categories in our communities—such as religious beliefs, socioeconomic demographics, the political climate, cultural values, and things of like manner. Why was this required? To ensure that we understood the mindset of the people we were trying to reach. This intel proved invaluable, as it helped me come to grips with people's presuppositions, values, beliefs, likes, and dislikes, which in turn helped me craft gospel-shaped messages that met people on their own turf. Similarly, churches today need to help their congregations become culturally savvy, by cracking the unique cultural code of their community. We're accustomed to our smartphones and computers frequently sending us software updates, right? Well, our congregations need periodic "thoughtware" updates to enable people to navigate—with a missional mindset—the fast-paced and ever-changing culture in which we live.

As we discussed in the previous chapter, one such belief shaping our current American culture is postmodern deconstructionism, whose adherents are actively attempting to dismantle what the modern era erected. Granted, some of these young, overly zealous activists marching the streets are totally clueless about the philosophy driving their vociferous activism. But hey, people seem passionate, so why not jump aboard?

Besides this burgeoning force to be reckoned with, American culture is increasingly marked by a colorful mosaic of diverse beliefs—a religious pluralism that includes the major world religions of Judaism, Christianity, and Islam, adherents to Hinduism and Buddhism, and virtually every other religion known to humanity.

Add to this the influence of spiritualism—including the occult, Wicca, New Age, and theosophy—as well as atheism, agnosticism, apatheism, and the growing numbers of nones.

All this to say that America represents a melting pot of beliefs.

Now, let me help you exhale a sigh of relief: I'm not implying that Christians need to understand all these belief systems, though they should understand the predominate beliefs at work in their immediate context. If you live in Southern California, you'll want to know something about the Church of Scientology. If you live in Hawaii, you'll want to be aware of the Buddhist mindset. If you live in Utah or Idaho, you'll want some understanding of Mormonism. You get my point. We must understand the specific context in which we live. The reason I spent extra time on postmodern deconstructionism is that its influence is seen systemically on a national level, whereas some of the beliefs listed above are often clustered in a particular area.

2. Churches with a missional mindset don't shy away from apologetics.

Shockingly, many pastors shun apologetics in their teaching. This is unfortunate. Admittedly, apologetics doesn't save anyone, but having the ability to defend the faith can offer Christians extra conversational confidence when they interact with unbelievers. Seen this way, a Christian trained in apologetics is equipped to help skeptics eliminate both their emotional and intellectual obstacles to belief. Apologetics can also help Christians—especially doubting ones—become more settled and confident in their faith.

Pastors shun apologetics for various reasons. Some avoid the topic altogether due to a bad experience with an apologist who was ultra-rigid or overly black-and-white, who treated people condescendingly or came across as harsh or arrogant. Other pastors avoid apologetics because they believe it overemphasizes the mind at the expense of the heart.

I'm sympathetic to these concerns. And I loathe how apologetics has sometimes been misused as a tool to bully people—ignoring matters of the heart and mentally incarcerating people in an ultra-tight denominational box. But that doesn't mean it's not a useful and valuable tool when used properly. I mean, how foolish would it be for a carpenter to never use a saw because he had seen one being misused? Similarly, we shouldn't throw out apologetics just because some Christians have misused it.

Not every Christian has to become an apologist, but every Christian should at least know the basics of how to give a defense of the Christian faith. Equipping every Christian with a few basic arguments can go a long way toward advancing the work of the gospel. Every church should teach some basic apologetics, including arguments for the existence of God, the reliability of the New Testament, and the resurrection of Jesus Christ. These three topics are both essential and a great place to start.

It's not difficult to get this going in your church. For example, you could invite an apologist to your church to speak about one of the three core topics. You can create a page on your church website with recommendations for some good apologetics podcasts, YouTube channels, and books.[2] You can identify people in your church who are already interested in apologetics and utilize them to develop an apologetics ministry to equip others in the congregation.

As a pastor, I tailor my weekly messages to allow for twenty minutes of Q&A at the end of each service. During this time, people are free to ask me questions about the message, other areas of the Bible, our church, apologetics, culture, philosophy, relationships, and morality. This Q&A time has become a vibrant part of our church culture and is a much-anticipated event each week. It lets people know that their questions, doubts, curiosities, and concerns are important and welcome. As a church, we grapple through issues together intellectually, and the people love it—because they know their voices matter!

3. Churches with a missional mindset equip their members with a Christian worldview.
Christianity is more than just a free pass to heaven. It's a way of life. Our faith in Jesus should influence every sphere of our

lives—from day-to-day living at home and at work, to politics, entertainment, technology, education, medicine, sports, music, and the arts. A proper Christian worldview teaches people how to perceive the world rightly, think Christianly, and make godly decisions in every aspect of life.

Worldview training should be interlaced through every ministry of the church, from the cradle to the grave. Through their participation in the church, people should gain a better understanding of how Christianity engages with culture. When we equip people with a Christian worldview, we reinforce the relevance of Christianity. A Christian worldview includes answers to questions such as, "Where did we come from?" "Why are we here?" "What's wrong with the world?" and "How do we go about fixing it?" It also helps us address cultural questions, such as "What does the Bible say about marriage? Sex? Alcohol? Relationships? Abortion?" Answering these questions allows us to view the world through a biblical lens.

4. Churches with a missional mindset help believers understand the power of social media and how to use it wisely.

One reason for the rapid change in our culture is the pervasive impact of social media. As Christians, we need to understand how algorithms work to customize our media feeds based on our likes and dislikes. If we become interested in a particular field or curious about an emerging issue, it won't be long before the platform picks up on that and starts feeding us more information about that topic.

This can be problematic. If we passively receive these messages, they will shape our worldview. This is one reason for the sharp political divide in our nation today. When we become stuck in our silos of self-interest, we lose our ability to see outside them. We can no longer hear each other because our perspective is constantly reinforced by the algorithms that have been customized for us based on our interests, likes, and dislikes. Awareness of what is happening behind the scenes can help us be more cautious about becoming trapped by algorithms that only seek to feed our biases.

The last thing we need is for Twitter, Instagram, TikTok, or Facebook to become the primary influence that shapes our worldview. To avoid this, we must equip our churches to use this technology wisely. It's no secret that people spend a lot more time on social media platforms than they do at church. We might as well help them use these platforms wisely by offering them a biblical way to view the world of social media.

5. Churches with a missional mindset help believers strategically share the gospel.

In times past, churches offered evangelism training that worked for that day and age; but we must now ask how we can most effectively share the gospel in our current day. For example, many behaviors that the church deemed sinful were also considered wrong in the culture at large. That made evangelism a lot easier. But all that has changed. Today, the government has legalized many behaviors once deemed sinful, and many people now consider these behaviors good.

We must become more strategic when sharing the gospel based on fallen humanity's need for a Savior, because people may not *feel* sinful.

What can we do?

Perhaps something like this: Next time you're in a conversation with someone who is celebrating an immoral lifestyle, ask what quality of life that lifestyle is producing. Here's what I can guarantee: It's not a life free of consequences. And that's what you want the person to see. You want to show people the connection between their behavior and the consequences that accrue. You can ask a simple question: "If living that way is so good, why are there so many negative consequences?"

Instead of trying to point out a person's sin, we can work backward, beginning with their self-acknowledged consequences. We can explain that the reason for the consequences is that they have bought in to a lie—the lie that evil is good. Many in our society celebrate abortion, adultery, divorce, drug use, same-sex attraction, pornography, and rejecting one's gender.

Calling such things *good* doesn't eliminate the consequences. The couple that has an abortion still feels guilty, as do people who commit adultery. People who get divorced still experience the shattering of their dreams and the consequences of a broken marriage. People who use drugs still get addicted. Believing that something is okay when it isn't does precious little to remove the feelings of guilt, nor will it eliminate the consequences. We can help people connect the dots by showing the value of living in sync with God's moral law, which subsequently leads to a life of blessing, minus the guilt and shame.

6. Churches with a missional mindset intentionally disciple their young people.

Imagine how difficult it will be for our young kids to someday pastor a church or live for Christ in this culture. It seems hard now, but it's only going to get harder. That's why we need to be very intentional in training our youth. Studies show that more pastors today are over sixty-five years of age than under forty. In 1992, only 6 percent of pastors were sixty-five or older, and 33 percent were forty or younger. By 2017, the numbers had changed to where 17 percent of pastors were sixty-five or older, and only 15 percent were forty or younger.[3]

With all that has changed since 2017, I can only imagine what the percentages look like today. These statistics are a startling reminder of why the church needs to be extra intentional in developing the next generation. But it will require keen insight into the kind of gospel *grit* this emerging generation will need in order to lead effectively. Chances are these future leaders will pay a much heavier price for their commitment to Christ than leaders of the past several generations. Our young people in the church need more than just fun and games; they need training to develop strength of character, maturity, and biblical literacy. The path will be difficult for every Christian wanting to live out his or her faith, but it will be especially hard for those leading the way. This emerging generation must learn and be reminded that this is a challenge worth taking.

7. Churches with a missional mindset help believers prepare to meet resistance.

Christianity is now deeply resented by many people in our culture. Those who are still willing to speak up and live for Jesus will increasingly face prejudice and perhaps even persecution in the years ahead. We have already seen hints of this, as Christians are being forced into the cultural mold of politically correct language, deconstructed values and mores, and increasing debate over sexuality, race relations, and politics, to name a few. The resistance may seem somewhat mild now, but we can imagine what it will be like once the emerging generation has the power to enforce their will.

It's going to take gospel grit to stand for Jesus in the age to come. Now is the time to remind people of Jesus' high-cost calling and his proactive preparation of his disciples to join him in carrying the cross.[4] It's time to bury the prosperity gospel and the Jesus-lite messages that naively suggest there's no cost to following Christ. The truth is that Jesus demands our *everything*. Now is not the time for low-bar discipleship. The bar must be raised, and we must gear up for resistance.

8. Churches with a missional mindset help believers refuse to be love-shamed.

Knowing that we are called to love the world as Jesus loved, Satan has craftily silenced many Christians by making them believe they are unloving if they express their beliefs. Countless Christians have thus been love-shamed into celebrating what God clearly condemns. Just because we disagree with or disapprove of what is happening in our culture doesn't mean we're unloving. This is especially true regarding the LGBTQ communities. Disagreeing with someone's lifestyle choices doesn't equate to not loving the person. This is a moral disagreement. We'd be wise to see through the rhetorical tactics used to get us to accommodate the ways of postmodern culture. We can love people and still disagree with them. That's what *tolerance* really means. We do this all the time in other areas of life. Everyone does.

9. Churches with a missional mindset exhort believers to speak up.

It seems that everyone is out of the closet today . . . except some Christians. It's time for the church to come out of hiding and stand unashamedly for the gospel.[5] The world doesn't want to hear what the church has to say. But we've been commissioned by our Lord Jesus to share the gospel, and we must do so, both humbly and wisely. The gospel was never meant to be a secret. As Jesus said to his followers, "You are the light of the world. A town built on a hill cannot be hidden. Neither do people light a lamp and put it under a bowl. Instead they put it on its stand, and it gives light to everyone in the house. In the same way, let your light shine before others, that they may see your good deeds and glorify your Father in heaven."[6]

Sharing the gospel is our Great Commission mandate. This doesn't have to be complicated, but sometimes we make it that way. At its core, evangelism is a *lifestyle*, not a program. Keep it simple: Live a life worthy of the gospel, and be ready to speak when needed.

We would do well to engage people organically with the gospel in our day-to-day interactions. This can be done by showing interest in the lives of the people we cross paths with, by asking them questions to initiate conversations. Again, keep it simple: "Where are you from? What brought you to the area? Do you like it here? What are your hobbies? How are you holding up lately? What do you like to do on the weekends? Do you have a church home?" Asking questions goes a long way when it comes to connecting the gospel to people's hearts. Unfortunately, many have lost the art of asking good questions.

When we ask questions, it tells people we're interested in them. When we take an interest in people's lives, they often return the favor and ask us questions as well. Sometimes, conversations like these can lead to great opportunities to share the gospel. The key is this: If you sense an open door to engage in spiritual conversation, walk through it. If you sense the door is closed or closing, give the person space and continue to focus on building your friendship. Sharing the gospel effectively boils down to some good old-fashioned people skills, coupled with a sensitivity to following the leading of the Holy Spirit. Remember, we're not called to cram the gospel down people's throats, but neither are we to keep it stuck in our own.

10. Churches with a missional mindset help believers engage the world without compromise.

One thing I love about Jesus is how he engaged with the world without being corrupted by it. As Christians, our goal is to imitate the life of Jesus by striving to act like him in everything we do, think, and say. We are his disciples, which means we take our cues from him. Of course, life can be slippery for all of us. But when we slip, we learn from the experience and rise again. God is so great that he can take our greatest mess-ups and use them as inspirational material to showcase how he has transformed our lives. We don't need to be perfect to be used by God, but we are looking *to* the perfection that is found in Jesus Christ. He exemplifies the picture-perfect life we are to emulate.

Unfortunately, the church has hit a rough patch in recent years, and there has been no shortage of moral and doctrinal compromise. To engage with the culture, many have lowered the bar to appeal to the proclivities of those they're trying to reach. Consequently, some churches have become indistinguishable from the culture. One thing about Jesus is that he never lowered the bar to reach people; rather, he set the bar even higher: "You have heard that it was said . . . but I tell you . . ."[7]

Regrettably, with so much compromise already in churches across the country, the church stands in desperate need of reformation if it intends to influence the world in the way that Jesus intends. It is to that topic we now turn.

Steps Toward a New Reformation

On October 31, 1517, Martin Luther nailed his Ninety-Five Theses to the door of the Castle Church in Wittenberg, Germany, codifying his concerns with the Catholic church. With one bold move,

Luther lit the match that sparked the Protestant Reformation. Having taken a few Reformation tours myself, and having stood at the door of the Castle Church, I can say this: If ever there was a time for a new reformation, that time is now.

There are several reasons why I say that the church in America is in shambles.

Some of the mess relates to the rapid changes in our culture that have tempted some churches to compromise the truth in order to fit in to society. Some of the chaos is the natural result of spoon-feeding the saints a watered-down diet, contributing to much of the doctrinal confusion among believers today. Some of the disorder stems from false teaching that has infiltrated the church. Adding to the mess are those who continue to participate in the church not to preserve it but to pervert it. Among these are some who would like to give the church a face-lift. To update it. To make it "culturally relevant." And, of course, the number of church scandals over the past few decades has made the mess seem nearly impossible to clean up. The church's story is a messy one. But it's the story in which we find ourselves.

Reformation Precedes Revival

When we look at the church in light of the prevailing culture, I can imagine some people saying, "Bobby, we don't need a *reformation*; we need a *revival*." I agree. The church *does* need revival. But before God revives his church again, I suspect he will sort us out through reformation first. That's because the church in America has all but lost its way. There's no sense reviving a church that is doctrinally, morally, and spiritually confused about what Christianity is. There's some sorting out to do, some reforming. And then, once we know who we are again—and, more importantly, who God is—we'll be a gospel-presenting body in which a revival would be more than welcome.

If you think about it, the European Reformation, in places like Germany, Switzerland, and England, all *preceded* the Great Awakening that swept across Europe and the United States in the eighteenth century. The truth is, we need both reformation *and* revival. Reformation without revival may simply lead to truth without power, whereas revival without reformation may lead to power without truth. For the church to take up its rightful place in the culture—that of salt and light—it needs to advance in truth *and* power. Through reformation, we straighten out our *minds*. Through revival, we straighten out our *hearts*. I realize there's overlap between the two, but the distinction can be helpful—and we need *both*. With that in mind, how can the church move forward in the direction of experiencing a new reformation? I understand there's a lot more to it, but here are four actions steps I'd like to challenge the church to take.

Actions Steps toward Reformation

1. Identify the problems in the church that need reforming.

Luther couldn't post his ninety-five theses without first reflecting on his contentions. I'm certainly not advocating for a long list, but we do need reform on the essentials of what makes up our Christian faith. Rallying around the gospel and the authority of Scripture is a good place to start. Due to our culture's embrace of all things LGBTQ, we would also be wise to unify around a biblical stance toward human sexuality—and especially how we can be a voice of compassion without compromise. We should aim for a *unifying statement* that addresses the top cultural issues of our day that threaten to undermine our Christian faith. Again, the list shouldn't be long, but it should be clear enough and broad enough to reach across the spectrum to help us stand together as the body of Christ during these trying times. Think of it like a manifesto of sorts, whereby leaders from various denominations work to develop a unifying creed in which they sign off historically on the Apostles' Creed and sign off culturally regarding some of the bigger issues confronting the church such as CRT, LGBTQ, progressive Christianity, sexual abuse, unchecked immoral leaders, and other such threats undermining the church from the inside and the outside.

2. Encourage bold and wise leaders to find ways to unify the church at large.

We are living in times that will require great courage of us. We need leaders to rise to the occasion and figure out ways to network us all together. Let history be a lesson for us. During the 1930s in Germany, the church was heavily compromised as Adolf Hitler sought to make the institution an instrument of his Nationalist Social party by forming a state church. To avoid hardship, many professed Christians went the way of the state, while those who sought to remain steadfast to God's Word found a way to band together. It was through courageous leaders such as Hanns Lilje, Martin Niemöller, Karl Barth, and Dietrich Bonhoeffer that the Confessing Church emerged. Essentially, there were two churches in Germany during this time: Hitler's Church (or what I'd call the Compromising Church) and the Confessing Church. We need courageous and visionary leaders to unify the confessing church in our day. That statement alone is challenging enough. But we need to figure out how to identify the true church as much as we can. For example, the splitting up of the United Methodist Church right now is an example of reform within a denomination. How to do this cross denominationally will be challenging, for sure, but we need to figure out a way to be more broadly unified as the church at large. No doubt, we will struggle to do this perfectly this side of heaven, but that shouldn't prevent gifted leaders from collaborating and brainstorming ways to bring us together. At heart, I'm not an alarmist. If anything, I'm a born optimist. But as a student of history and culture, I'd be remiss not to warn the church that the time is now to call for leaders to start rallying the troops. We'll be stronger together as a result.

*3. Break the silence and start using our voices
as agents of change.*

For too long, the church has been silent in the face of cultural regression. The same pattern was evident in pre-war Germany, where many naively thought nothing of what was happening . . . until it was too late. Though I'm not suggesting that anything on the order of concentration camps is in our future, I am concerned that Christians will be forced into silence to comply with the heavy-handed agenda that is seemingly gaining momentum in our country. We need to use our voices while we still have them. If ever there was a time to express your voice and vote your conscience at the ballot box, that time is now. Why wait until it's too late?

When you do speak up, people who oppose Christianity may try to tear you down. In calling for the church to speak up, I'm certainly not suggesting we become obnoxious or lose our Christian witness. I'm just warning against *passivity*. God knows there's enough of that in the church already.

4. Recognize that reformation comes at a cost.

Reformation is never easy, and I suspect there is much adversity ahead. But let's not squander the opportunity to steer the ship in the right direction. Yes, the church is in bad shape, but that only means we must do some spiritual exercise to get us back in transformational shape. It's time to turn to God in heartfelt prayer, explore our hearts and confess our sins, and ask God to help us renew our commitment to him so that we can be the witnesses that Christ calls us to be. The times are dark, but we've been given an opportunity to shine. The darker the culture becomes, the more brightly our light can shine. It's certainly not easy watching what is happening both inside and outside the church, but we can rejoice knowing that the true bride of Christ is still around. We just need to work together prayerfully to bring about a new reformation. So, let's develop some gospel grit and get after it.

NOTES

FOREWORD
1. John Steinbeck, *East of Eden*, Steinbeck Centennial Edition (New York: Penguin, 2002), 444.

INTRODUCTION
1. Matthew 16:18, NLT.

WHY ARE THERE SO MANY SCANDALS IN THE CHURCH?
1. Matthew 7:21.

AREN'T CHRISTIANS JUST A BUNCH OF HYPOCRITES?
1. Adapted from Ezgi Özeke Kocabaş and Meltem Üstündağ-Budak, "Validation Skills in Counselling and Psychotherapy," *International Journal of Scientific Study* 5, no. 8 (November 2017): 320.
2. Mark 7:6.

WHY DON'T CHURCHES HOLD THEIR LEADERS ACCOUNTABLE?
1. Brandon Ambrosino, "'Someone's Gotta Tell the Freakin' Truth': Jerry Falwell's Aides Break Their Silence," *Politico*, September 9, 2019, https://www.politico.com/magazine/story/2019/09/09/jerry-falwell-liberty-university-loans-227914/. Italics in the original.
2. Will Maule, "News Analysis," *Premier Christianity*, March 25, 2021, https://www.premierchristianity.com/the-fall-of-ravi-zacharias/3918.article.
3. Ephesians 4:15.
4. 1 Samuel 2:12-17, 22-36.
5. 1 Timothy 5:19.

6. 1 Timothy 5:20.
7. Matthew 18:15-17.

WHY DO CHRISTIANS USE GOD'S NAME TO OPPRESS OTHERS?
1. Friedrich Nietzsche, *Twilight of the Idols or How to Philosophize with the Hammer* [1889], trans. Richard Polt (Indianapolis: Hackett, 1997), 54.
2. Karl Marx, "A Contribution to the 'Critique' . . . Introduction," in *Critique of Hegel's "Philosophy of Right,"* trans. Annette Jolin and Joseph O'Malley, ed. Joseph O'Malley (Cambridge, UK: Cambridge University Press, 1970), 131.

DOES GOD REALLY CARE ABOUT MY GENDER IDENTITY?
1. Iris Jung, "Oli London detransitions from 'Korean' woman to British man," Yahoo News, November 14, 2022, https://news.yahoo.com/oli -london-detransitions-korean-woman-001720404.html.
2. Edie Heipel, "De-transitioner Oli London shares conversion to Christianity," *Catholic News Agency*, November 4, 2022, https://www .catholicnewsagency.com/news/252732/de-transitioner-oli-london -shares-conversion-to-christianity.
3. Genesis 1:27; Psalm 139:13-17.

WHY ARE SO MANY CHRISTIANS RACISTS?
1. Acts 17:26, ESV.
2. Genesis 1:27.
3. Genesis 9:6.
4. James 3:9-10.
5. Acts 10:15.
6. Galatians 2:11-16.
7. Galatians 3:28.
8. John 3:16; italics added.

DOESN'T CHRISTIANITY DEVALUE WOMEN?
1. Matthew 28:1-10; Mark 16:1-8; Luke 24:1-10; John 19:25-27; 20:11-18.
2. Ephesians 5:21.
3. Ephesians 5:22.
4. Ephesians 5:25.
5. John 10:30.
6. John 15:13; Ephesians 5:25; 6:4.

WHY ARE CHRISTIANS SO OBSESSED WITH PRO-LIFE?
1. Psalm 139:13-16.
2. Lawrence B. Finer et al., "Reasons US Women Have Abortions: Quantitative and Qualitative Perspectives," *Perspectives on Sexual and*

Reproductive Health 37, no. 3 (September 2005): 113, https://pubmed
.ncbi.nlm.nih.gov/16150658/.

3. Jeremiah 1:5; italics added.
4. Psalm 51:5; italics added.
5. Exodus 21:22-25.
6. Luke 1:39-45.
7. Luke 2:12, 16.
8. Psalm 139:14.
9. 1 John 1:5, 9.

WHY DO CHRISTIANS MAKE SO MANY EXCUSES FOR GOD?

1. Richard Dawkins, *The God Delusion* (Boston: Houghton Mifflin,
   2006), 31.
2. "Why do Christians make so many excuses for their god," r/exchristian,
   reddit.com, comment by averjam, accessed June 7, 2023, https://www
   .reddit.com/r/exchristian/comments/s3txi3/why_do_christians_make
   _so_many_excuses_for_their/.
3. 1 Peter 3:15.

HOW CAN A GOOD GOD ALLOW US TO SUFFER?

1. Matthew 28:20.

HOW CAN JESUS BE THE ONLY WAY TO HEAVEN WHEN SO MANY HAVE NEVER HEARD OF HIM?

1. John 14:6.

HOW CAN A LOVING GOD SEND PEOPLE TO HELL?

1. Romans 1:20.
2. 2 Peter 3:9, NKJV.
3. C. S. Lewis, *The Great Divorce: A Dream* (New York: HarperOne, 2001),
   75.

DOES THE RISE OF THE NONES MEAN THE INSTITUTIONAL CHURCH IS OBSOLETE?

1. Gregory A. Smith, "About Three-in-Ten US Adults Are Now Religiously
   Unaffiliated," Pew Research Center, December 14, 2021, https://www
   .pewresearch.org/religion/2021/12/14/about-three-in-ten-u-s-adults-are
   -now-religiously-unaffiliated/.
2. Ryan Burge, "Religious disaffiliation is rising. Is there a path back to
   the fold?" *Deseret News*, March 24, 2021, https://www.deseret.com
   /indepth/2021/3/24/22348276/the-power-of-one-religious-nones
   -unaffiliated-atheist-agnostic-belief-in-god.
3. Hebrews 10:25, NLT.

4. Luke 9:23.
5. Matthew 16:18, ESV.
6. John 10:3-4, 14.
7. Matthew 9:37-38.

CAN'T I BE SPIRITUAL WITHOUT BEING A CHRISTIAN?

1. Caroline Kitchener, "What It Means To Be Spiritual But Not Religious," *The Atlantic*, January 11, 2018, https://www.theatlantic.com/membership /archive/2018/01/what-it-means-to-be-spiritual-but-not-religious /550337/.
2. 1 Corinthians 2:13-14.

ISN'T SCIENCE ABOUT FACTS AND RELIGION ABOUT FAITH?

1. Kenneth D. Boa and Robert M. Bowman Jr., *Faith Has Its Reasons: An Integrative Approach to Defending Christianity* (Colorado Springs: NavPress, 2001).
2. Baruch Aba Shalev, *100 Years of Nobel Prizes* (New Delhi: Atlantic Publishers, 2003), 57.
3. Shalev, *100 Years of Nobel Prizes*, 57. Shalev notes that "atheists, agnostics, and freethinkers comprise 10.5% of total Nobel Prize winners; but in the category of Literature, these preferences rise sharply to about 35%."

HASN'T ATHEISM BURIED GOD?

1. "Thales of Miletus (c. 620 BCE –c. 546 BCE)," *Internet Encyclopedia of Philosophy*, https://iep.utm.edu/thales/#H3.
2. "Anaximenes (d. 528 BCE)," *Internet Encyclopedia of Philosophy*, https:// iep.utm.edu/anaximenes/.
3. "Heraclitus (fl. c. 500 BCE)," *Internet Encyclopedia of Philosophy*, https:// iep.utm.edu/heraclit/.
4. Richard Dawkins, *The Blind Watchmaker: Why the Evidence of Evolution Reveals a Universe without Design* (New York: W. W. Norton, 1996), 10.
5. David Baggett and Jerry L. Walls, *God and Cosmos: Moral Truth and Human Meaning* (New York: Oxford University Press, 2016), 23.
6. John 10:10. For an encouraging look at the many verses in the Bible that speak of the abundant life, see https://www.openbible.info/topics /abundant_life.

IS THERE RELIABLE EVIDENCE FOR GOD'S EXISTENCE?

1. Bertrand Russell, quoted in Thomas Kelly, "Evidence," *The Stanford Encyclopedia of Philosophy* (Winter 2016), Edward N. Zalta (ed.), https:// plato.stanford.edu/entries/evidence/.

2. I don't know *where* or *when* Pascal said this, but two thousand online quote sites can't all be wrong . . . can they? I suppose they can, but not likely.

3. Richard C. Lewontin, "Billions and Billions of Demons," *The New York Review*, January 9, 1997, 31.

4. For more, see these resources: Kenneth D. Boa and Robert M. Bowman Jr., *20 Compelling Evidences That God Exists: Discover Why Believing in God Makes So Much Sense* (Tulsa, OK: RiverOak, 2002), and W. David Beck, *Does God Exist? A History of Answers to the Question* (Downers Grove, IL: IVP Academic, 2021).

5. For more on Craig's work on the Kalam, in both popular and scholarly arenas, visit www.reasonablefaith.org/writings, where you can access his argument and responses to his critics.

6. Psalm 19:1.

7. JOC Team, "Anthropic Principle—What Is It and Could It Be True?" *Journal of Cosmology*, December 9, 2021, https://journalofcosmology.com/anthropic100.html.

8. See Hugh Ross, *The Fingerprint of God*; Fred Heeren, *Show Me God*; and William Dembski, *Mere Creation*.

9. C. S. Lewis, *Mere Christianity* (New York: HarperOne, 2015), 29.

10. Romans 2:14-15.

11. David Baggett and Jerry L. Walls wrote a fascinating three-part trilogy on the moral law—all published by Oxford University Press: *Good God: The Theistic Foundations of Morality* (2011), *God and Cosmos: Moral Truth and Human Meaning* (2016), and *The Moral Argument: A History* (2019).

12. Robert Conway, "Christian Theism and the Problem of Guilt," (doctoral thesis, University of Birmingham, September 2020), https://etheses.bham.ac.uk/id/eprint/11472/7/Conway2021PhD.pdf. See chapter 23 for my argument from moral guilt.

13. See my book *The Fifth Gospel: Matthew, Mark, Luke, John, . . . You* (Eugene, OR: Harvest House, 2014), which I wrote specifically to show how our lives can serve as an apologetic before a watching world.

HOW CAN PEOPLE BELIEVE IN MIRACLES TODAY?

1. Frank Turek, *Stealing from God: Why Atheists Need God to Make Their Case* (Colorado Springs: NavPress, 2014), 189. Italics added.

2. Genesis 1:1.

3. Matthew 28; Mark 16; Luke 24; John 20.

4. 1 Corinthians 15:14.

DID JESUS *REALLY* RISE FROM THE DEAD?

1. 1 Corinthians 15:17, esv.

2. Paul E. Little, *Know Why You Believe* (Wheaton, IL: Scripture Press, 1967), 28.
3. Charles Colson, quoted in Marty Angelo, "How Chuck Colson's Legacy of Hope Lives On," Prison Fellowship, https://www.prisonfellowship.org /2018/04/chuck-colsons-legacy-hope-lives/.
4. 1 Corinthians 15:1-7.
5. See John 21.
6. See Matthew 16:21; Mark 14:58; Luke 9:22; John 2:19.
7. 1 Corinthians 15:3-4, ESV.
8. John 20:27-28; Acts 9:1-9; 1 Corinthians 15:5-8.

WHY CHRISTIANITY STILL MAKES SENSE TO ME
1. 1 Corinthians 15:17.
2. Romans 8:16.
3. Luke 18:17.
4. John 10:9; italics added.

AFTERWORD: A WAY FORWARD FOR THE CHURCH
1. 1 Peter 3:15.
2. There are so many great resources to choose from, but here are a few to get you started. First, if you enjoy podcasts, I encourage you to check out William Lane Craig's *Defenders Podcast*, *The Alisa Childers Podcast*, and *The Natasha Crain Podcast*. On YouTube, be sure to check out Frank Turek's *Cross-Examined* channel; Mike Winger's channel; and *THE BEAT by Allen Parr*. Finally, if you're looking for a few good apologetics books, see Timothy Keller, *The Reason for God: Belief in an Age of Skepticism* (Penguin, 2008), J. Warner Wallace, *Cold-Case Christianity: A Homicide Detective Investigates the Claims of the Gospels* (David C. Cook, 2013), and Nancy Pearcey, *Total Truth: Liberating Christianity from Its Cultural Captivity* (Crossway, 2008).
3. "The Aging of America's Pastors," Barna, March 1, 2017, https://www .barna.com/research/aging-americas-pastors/.
4. Luke 9:23.
5. Romans 1:16.
6. Matthew 5:14-16.
7. Matthew 5:17-48.

ABOUT THE AUTHOR

Hi, friend. I'm Bobby. I grew up in the land of fruits and nuts. That's right, you guessed it: California! If I had to give you a list of words to describe me before I became a Christian, it would include *insecure, angry, confused, uneducated, promiscuous, boozer, addict, foolish, rebellious,* and *a decent baseball player.* Obviously, this was a recipe for disaster. When I was nineteen, a college baseball teammate took me to hear evangelist Greg Laurie. His message resonated with me, and soon I became a follower of Jesus.

After becoming a Christian and cleaning up my life, I developed such a passion for God that I couldn't imagine doing anything but full-time ministry. I hung up my baseball cleats and headed off to Bible college in Conway, Arkansas. During my time there, I served as a staff evangelist and a teaching pastor. With a desire to be further trained for ministry, I enrolled at Dallas Theological Seminary and earned a master's in theology. I also earned a DMin in apologetics from Southern Evangelical Seminary and a PhD in philosophy of religion from the University of Birmingham in England.

Since 1996, I've been married to Heather, and together we have two grown children: Haley and Dawson. Heather and I enjoyed speaking at Family Life's Weekend to Remember marriage retreats for nearly ten years, and today I serve as lead pastor at Image Church in Charlotte, North Carolina, while also running a YouTube channel, *Christianity Still Makes Sense* (formerly *One Minute Apologist*). In addition, I cohost a nationally syndicated radio show called *Pastors' Perspective*, a call-in program where people can ask their questions about God and the Bible. My hobbies include date nights with my bride, family time with our kids, traveling, and reading thought-provoking books.

JOIN BOBBY CONWAY IN FINDING HOPE AMIDST A CULTURE OF DOUBT

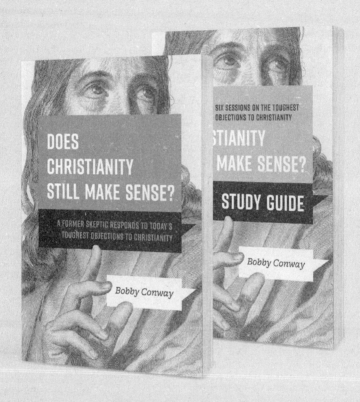

In his book *Does Christianity Still Make Sense?*, Bobby Conway helps readers respond to the greatest questions to the Christian faith, based on his own experience with doubt.

The *Does Christianity Still Make Sense? Study Guide* explores a wealth of compelling evidence in favor of Christianity that is worth unpacking in six interactive sessions.

Available wherever books are sold.